ADV.

"The books are indispensable travel companion for first timers, a must for regulars and, for the amount of golden nuggets and heaps of cherished information contained, vital for the downright lunatic Italophiles. Let's give the authors credit for having had the capacity to dig into the substrata of the region's soul, turn them upside down and inside out and hash out without presumption a bounty of surprise hints that can only be fruit of someone that has a very special bond and love relation with Italy. *Eccellente amici miei!*"

— **DARIO CASTAGNO**, author of "Too Much Tuscan Sun"

"Zeneba Bowers and Matt Walker convey the real Italy, the day-to-day routines of its people and the tastes of its culinary traditions. They deliver what every armchair traveler and guidebook devotee is seeking: An indelible sense of place and the locals-only advice you need to experience it for yourself."

— **ROBERT FIRPO-CAPPIELLO**, Editor in Chief, Budget Travel (BudgetTravel.com)

"Peace, authenticity and timelessness — the perfect travel philosophy."

— **CATHERINE MARIEN**, founder of "Slow Italy"

Tuscany
I T A L Y

*Small-town Itineraries for
the Foodie Traveler*

Zeneba Bowers
Matt Walker

Note: Since this is a "Kindle MatchBook" you can download the Amazon Kindle for free, along with any updates, delivered automatically.

Tuscany, Italy
Small-town Itineraries for the Foodie Traveler

Zeneba Bowers & Matt Walker

S E C O N D E D I T I O N

ISBN: 978-1-942545-37-8
Library of Congress Control Number: 2015959342

All photography by Zeneba Bowers and Matt Walker.
Maps by Laura Atkinson. Book design by Nancy Cleary.

Although the authors and publisher have made every effort to ensure that the information in this book was correct at the time of publication, neither the authors nor Little Roads LLC assume any liability to any party for any loss, damage, or disruption caused by errors or omissions.

Little Roads Publishing
An Imprint of Wyatt-MacKenzie

www.LittleRoadsEurope.com

Table of Contents

Southern Tuscany
Monte Amiata and the Val d'Orcia

Southern Tuscany
Around Pienza

MILANO

VENEZIA

BOLOGNA

FIRENZE

TOSCANA →

SIENA

ROMA

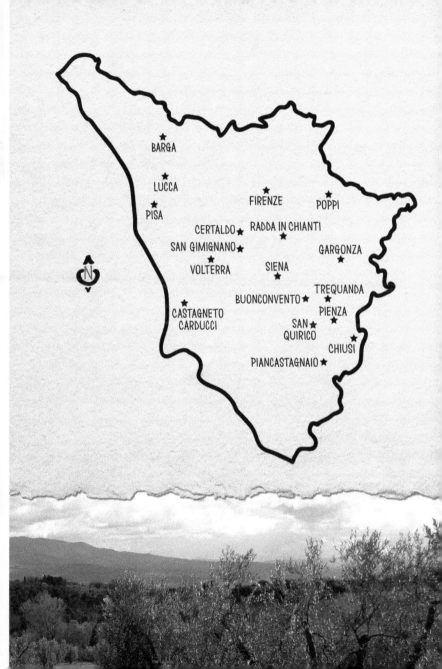

OUR GOALS

Wherever we travel, our goals are always the same:

★ Adapting to the culture and interacting with the locals;

★ Experiencing life beyond what one finds as a typical tourist;

★ Slowing down and allowing ourselves time to take in everything around us;

★ Learning about the food, culture and history of the area; and

★ Avoiding tourist crowds whenever possible.

ABOUT THIS BOOK

We have visited Italy over 50 times in the past ten years, and we even recently bought a little apartment there. In our travels, we have been drawn again and again to various parts of Tuscany. With hundreds of travel guides covering Tuscany to choose from, why read this one?

We find unusual sights, great local restaurants, masterful artisans, and unique lodging, many of which have little or no presence on the Internet or in guidebooks. Unlike other guidebooks, we generally skip the bigger places like Florence and Siena, and instead delve deeply into the heart of the countryside.

This book contains seven driving itineraries, covering different and diverse regions of Tuscany. These itineraries are very loose, designed to allow you to go at your own pace, rather than giving specific day-by-day direction. We advise allowing 3-7 days for each one, and even more time if you have it. Some of them will easily overlap with one another, and the routes to the north can be combined with routes from our other guidebooks to Emilia Romagna and the northern Alpine lakes of Italy. They will guide you through some of the most beautiful countryside, take you to some fascinating locations, and lead you to some of the most delicious food and drink experiences you'll ever find.

At the end of each itinerary you'll find listings of the restaurants, lodgings, sights and artisans mentioned in the chapter. We provide websites where possible, though some of the lodgings have no website, but only listings on booking sites.

Regarding road maps: There are many ways to navigate these little roads that we love to travel. Many people like to use GPS or various mapping apps for their phones; others prefer a good old-fashioned road map, complete with the fun of folding the thing thousands of times until the paper wears out. Detailed road maps of Tuscany are easily found online, at airport bookstores, and at service stations in Italy.

To help you get a rough idea of where things are, each itinerary begins with a rough map of the area it covers.

Overwhelmed by the prospect of planning an Italian trip?

Little Roads Europe *offers travel consulting and itinerary building services. We've created the Italian trip of a lifetime for many happy clients.*

Find out more at www.LittleRoadsEurope.com

FOOD: It's the Whole Point, After All

Much of traditional Tuscan cuisine is based on "*cucina povera*", or peasant cooking. The food comes from the land: in the case of Tuscany, the land is rocky, relatively dry, and heavily forested. Olives and grapes thrive in this environment, as do herbs, beans, and chestnuts; consequently, these things are prominent in Tuscan kitchens. Some dishes are meant to use leftover food, like *ribollita*, a soup made from yesterday's bread whose name literally means "re-boiled".

Tuscan bread, by the way, is typically made without salt; centuries of folklore give varying reasons for this, from prohibitive salt tax to rivalries between Florence and Pisa. In any case, the relatively bland bread is meant to complement the highly seasoned food. There is also the tradition of "*fare la scarpetta*" — literally, "to make the little shoe": This refers to the practice of using a piece of bread to mop up the remaining sauce from your plate or bowl — preferable to licking it like a dog, which you'll sometimes be tempted to do.

Today, Tuscan cuisine has achieved an exalted status among food lovers, but it is based in these peasant roots. Understanding these roots is the key to appreciating the food of the region, from the simplest kitchen dishes to the most elaborate plate presentations.

Here are a few food elements to look for:

Cinghiale - wild boar, in the form of sauces, *salumi*, or just roasted meat; common in the hilly, forested areas like Chianti and Monte Amiata.

Pecorino - sheeps' cheese, a specialty of Pienza in particular, though found throughout the region.

Cinta senese - pork specifically from the distinctive belted pigs of the Sienese region.

Olio - olive oil. An ubiquitous ingredient throughout Italy, of course; in Tuscany you'll drive by many farms that sell it directly ("*vendita diretta*").

Vino - especially the wines of Chianti, and Brunello di Montalcino, though any "*vino della casa*" will be great, and it will be specially selected to go with the food of the house.

Finocchio - fennel, used in many dishes, served raw in salads.

Fegatini - a good term to know if you don't like chicken liver. Often served on a *crostini* in paté form.

Castagne - chestnuts. Especially common in the forested hills and mountainous areas, often made into some great soup. Monte Amiata is famous for them.

Fagioli (beans), *tartufo* (truffles), *pici* (hand-rolled pasta), just a few of the very typical and much-loved foods in Tuscany.

Bistecca fiorentina - Florentine steak, made from the famously delicious *Chianina* breed. (You'll see these white cows in small herds as you drive through the hills and valleys of Tuscany.) This dish is priced by the kilogram, and it is a HUGE cut of meat — some three fingers thick. It is prepared on a grill and served VERY rare. For lovers of rare steaks, this is your holy grail.

In general, any grilled beef dish (*"manzo"*) in Tuscany will be served quite rare. This is the "right" way, and it's not advisable to ask for it well-done. If you're not a fan of really red beef, try one of the meat dishes prepared *"in umido"* (stewed), which will be cooked thoroughly. The same goes for lamb dishes.

We discuss all of these foodstuffs variously throughout the book.

A note on tipping: Each meal will include a per-person *coperto* (cover charge) on the bill (*"il conto"*). This is typically a couple of bucks, and is meant to stand the place of a tip. Though it's not generally expected, we always leave a little something extra to show appreciation for good service.

Planning a Trip to Tuscany

When planning a trip to Italy, the typical tendency is to cover as much ground as possible and see the most important sights — The Leaning Tower, the Colosseum, Venice, the Last Supper. We encourage you to throw out that checklist, as it is the same list as that of thousands of other tourists. An overly-packed schedule is a harsh mistress; if you want a minute-by-minute to-do list, you could have stayed at work. If you want an authentic experience, you need to allow yourself time to have one: Time to have a long lunch, to converse with locals, to explore a side street or an unexpected sight, to relax and breathe.

As itinerary planners, we have talked many clients out of some of the "must-see" destinations in favor of little-known places. They always return rested, fulfilled, and carrying life-long memories of their experiences.

The excursions in this book will guide you through some of the most beautiful countryside, take you to some fascinating locations, and lead you to some of the most delicious food and drink experiences you'll ever find.

Our way of traveling is different.

As professional classical musicians, Zeneba and Matt were founding members of the Grammy-nominated ALIAS Chamber Ensemble. We put a great deal of time and thought into creating interesting and diverse programs for concerts. By the time we founded the group, we had already performed much of the standard and often-heard music by famous composers. We decided to try something more adventurous. As a result the ensemble made a name for itself for commissioning new music, finding and performing great but unusual pieces by little-known composers, and occasionally offering lesser-known works by the great masters. The result became an eclectic concert experience that has something for everyone, while introducing audiences to new ways of listening to music.

When we started traveling to Europe, we applied the same general idea to our travel philosophy: After checking off the obligatory visits to the A-list locations (the Roman Colosseum, the Tower of London, Venice, Stonehenge, and the like), we started looking for more authentic, out-of-the-way experiences. We found them down the little roads of Europe — the small towns, the remote abbeys and castles, the ruins of Roman outposts, and of course the Grandma's-kitchen cuisine. This was a more immersive experience, visiting places without tourists but rich with culture, art, architecture, history, and food.

Little Roads Europe

PROLOGUE

A Day Immersed in Tuscany

Early morning in the small Tuscan hill town of Pienza: We stroll along the cliff walkway overlooking the Val d'Orcia, a region known for its panoramic beauty, its iconic winding cypress-lined roads, its huge influence on centuries of artists and writers.

Voices echo quietly off of the ancient city walls as the people go about their business. Donatella carrying her shopping bags home from the grocers, stopping to glare disapprovingly at Marcello and Luciano as they stand at the bar facing the town square.

Sitting with our first *cappuccini* of the day, we observe the two old men: Workers, already dusty from their early morning labors, both wearing their requisite rumpled Italian caps. Without a word, Marcello slides a 1€ coin across the bar to the barista. She serves them a pink, fizzy drink in a tiny glass, which they consume standing at the bar, in one practiced gulp. When they finish, they leave with a gruff *"Grazie, ciao"* — thanks, see ya — and return to whatever work precipitated their thirst. We ask the barista what the drink was; she tells us they call it a *"macchiatino"*. The name, normally meant to describe a coffee beverage, is probably an inside joke, as it turns out to be *prosecco* and *aperol*, otherwise known as a "spritz". It's very common for some of the local guys to have a couple of these in the morning with — or perhaps instead of — their coffee.

We note the time — 9:15 am — but, wanting to fit in, we order one for each of us. It turns out the old guys were right: This was a great start to the day.

Later we stop in at Valerio Trufelli's tiny leather workshop. Valerio has been crafting high-quality leather goods for something like half a century. We bought a wallet here 6 years ago which is now just getting soft and buttery; on this visit we decided to get a couple of his key fobs with our initials stitched into them. We tell him the initials we want — M and Z — and though he has neither of these letters already made, he offers to make them for us. We tell him which colors we want, but he shakes his head. "*No,*" he says, holding up a different color leather strip and stitching, "*questi colori sono meglio*" — these colors are better.

We return a couple of hours after lunch and he has them finished, and indeed his color choice seems perfect.

This is the lesson for traveling in Europe. Immerse yourself in the place, find out what's local, how things are done, what it feels like to just be there, to live there. Emulate the people of these storied cultures doing things their way, be it wine or art or food. Especially the food.

Early evening. We get a bottle of *prosecco,* a piece of cheese from one of the *pecorino* shops, and a hunk of fresh bread from the bakery; walk down to the footpath that traverses the cliffside just outside the Renaissance-era town gate; take a seat on a bench, and start to enjoy the evening. A few minutes later, Valerio the leather guy comes our way, on a rickety old bicycle. He stops, happy to chat with a customer, and together we take in the sunset over the valley as it lights up the distant slopes of Monte Amiata. He waves his hand with pride across the panorama like an old-fashioned show presenter, and proudly announces: "*Signore e Signori: La Val d'Orcia!*" — Ladies and Gentlemen: The Orcia Valley!

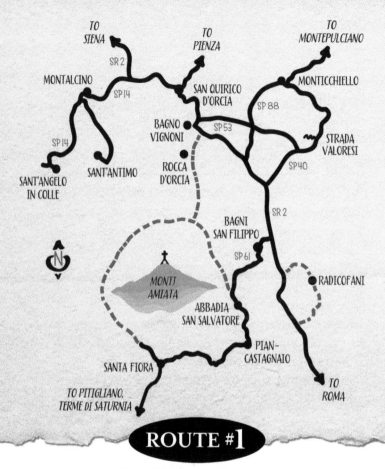

ROUTE #1

Southern Tuscany
Monte Amiata and the Val d'Orcia

*This route begins on the shoulders of the formerly volcanic **Monte Amiata** in southern Tuscany. The villages here have never grown to be very large because of the terrain, so many of them retain their old, small-town charm.*

Abbadia San Salvatore is the site of an 8th century abbey with a spookily-lit and otherworldly subterranean crypt. (Note: We are not responsible for any possessions and/or hauntings associated with your visit here.) The town's confusingly winding streets and one-way lanes lead to a lot of U-turns, but once you get sorted and park the car you can wander through the streets of its *centro storico* (historic center), which feels like a step back into time about 600 years. As a bonus, the relative difficulty pays off with a distinct lack of tourist crowds. The town is also home to the shop of **Aurelio Visconti**, who makes fantastic *liquori*; more adventurous travelers can seek out the store, while the less ambitious can proceed to Piancastagnaio, where several of their bottles are available at Ristorante Anna (which we'll visit in a bit).

Alternatively, stop by **Santa Fiora**, a small medieval town on the south side of the mountain, where you can find some very special artisanal foodstuffs at **Queste Terre Alimenti Tipici**, on the main square. Francesco Colitto keeps an interesting collection of local *liquori*, hand-made soaps, local honey, wine (of course!) and more. You can also dine in the casual, locally famous **Il Barilotto** restaurant, where unmarked bottles of *vino* sit on the table; drink as much as you wish (or as little —

is that a thing?). You pay only for what you've con-sumed. When we had lunch there, we went along with what the locals seemed to be ordering: The special of the day, a house-made potato-filled ravioli topped with a wild boar sauce (*ragu di cinghiale*).

Cinghiale — Tuscany's wild boar

One of Tuscany's most dangerous foods: *Cinghiale* are large, ferocious wild boar, weighing sometimes 400 pounds. They are hunted for meat and also for protection — they can often be destructive to vineyards and other croplands. Autumn is hunting season; in remote, forested areas, the *cacciatori* (hunters) can be seen in early mornings, preparing their guns and their dogs. In these instances travelers are better off abandoning their plans to hike through the woods, and instead find the nearest *ristorante* that might be serving some very fresh meat dishes later that day.

For our *secondi* (meat course), we made the mistake of trying to describe just how we wanted our beef fillet cooked; the result was an unfortunate plate of overdone meat.

This brings us to a lesson in Italian meat dishes: Most places won't ask you "How do you want that cooked?" They will bring it to you the "right" way. To ask for it otherwise marks you for a *straniero* (a dang foreigner), one who is not appreciative of their fine cuisine developed over many generations. Generally, beef in Italy is cooked rare or medium rare at most; if you don't like your steak a good bit bloody, stick to the pastas. It's not Burger King, so just let them do it their way. Wherever we travel, we've found that it's best to immerse ourselves in the way they do things there, whether it's food and drink, driving, or just generally passing the time. It's how memories are made.

The best dining in the area, as well as some nice sightseeing, is found in the town of **Piancastagnaio**. This small walled city is well worth a look around, though surrounded by a small amount of modern sprawl. In one of these newer strips, not far outside the north wall gate, is **Ristorante Anna**, one of the most memorable places you'll ever dine. It's not upscale, but the fresh and homemade quality of the food is outstanding: Beautifully delicate pastas, delicious soups, amazing desserts (their *crema catalana* is served on fire). The casualness with which the folks at Anna produce top-quality food is truly remarkable.

Ristorante Anna is a family-run, very local-oriented place. A large mural inside depicts the family matriarch as a young woman. Lunch reservations are recommended, especially on a Sunday, when most of the tables are pushed together and entire soccer teams, band groups, or families rent the whole restaurant. Sunday lunch is served family style: the dishes come out on large platters and the soup comes out in a huge copper tureen; they serve you a portion and move on to the next person. There are no menus; the owner just comes to the table to tell you what is available. Fresh, handmade pasta is always on offer, as well as daily soups. We have driven directly from the airport to get here for lunch specifically for their chestnut and mushroom soup.

Chestnuts from Amiata

Chestnuts are a staple food in many regions of Italy. Those from the densely-wooded slopes of Monte Amiata in Tuscany are some of the most highly regarded in Italy, carrying the IGP (*Indicazione Geografica Protetta*) designation. In lean times, the large forests of Tuscany produced a wealth of chestnuts which played a vital part in the food supply. Today Tuscany is still about 50% forested; chestnuts and chestnut flour find its way onto regional menus in everything from soup to, well, nuts.

For millennia, the slopes of Amiata have been the prime source of what are regarded as the best chestnuts in Italy. (In fact the town's name is derived from the Italian word for chestnuts, *castagne*.) Many of the restaurants in this region prepare multiple dishes using liberal quantities of chestnuts; after ten years of traveling, we think Anna's soup is still the best we've had anywhere. They also serve a chestnut grappa, *Marroncino*, a delicious finish to the meal. If they have extra bottles (assuming we haven't snatched them all up first), they may even sell you one to take home with you.

To the south of Piancastagnaio and Santa Fiora lie a couple of notable locations: The picturesque hot springs of **Terme di Saturnia** draws crowds seeking healing waters or just a chance to show of their beach bods. Tourists hit the fancy spas, while locals hit the free, ancient open-air thermal baths.

Nearby is the walled hilltop town of **Pitigliano**, its buildings clinging to the face of the cliff overlooking the valleys below. Sometimes referred to as "Little Jerusalem", this town was for centuries a haven for Jews who were escaping persecution from papal Rome and other parts of Europe's power structures. Its Synagogue was founded in 1598 and became the center of a rich heritage of Jewish culture and history.

At one ugly point in the town's development (around 1620), city officials used sticks to bang on the doors of Jewish homes — this was a notice of eviction, and they were forced to move to the "Jewish quarter" of town. In response, Jewish bakers created a sweet treat in stick form to honor (or mock) that history. It looks like a breadstick and is called *sfratti* — literally, "evicted". Made with honey and nuts, it's now a widespread and delicious staple of southern Tuscany's cuisine.

Near Pitigliano's historic ghetto, the excellent **Hostaria del Ceccottino** offers a menu based in part on Jewish culinary traditions, for those wishing to experience history on a plate.

The town's *centro storico* (historic center) is an extensive warren of ancient streets and interesting architecture, including a number of butcher shops. On one small side street, shop owners take pride in whimsically decorating their storefronts — many windows display stuffed wild boars wearing sunglasses, hats, shirts, and other people-clothes, often accompanied by fanciful lighting and disco balls.

Continuing north from Piancastagnaio, you'll come across another warm springs location in the forested foothills: **Bagni San Filippo**. Here again, a few spas offer luxury for a high price; but a walk through the woods from the tiny village leads to the Fosso Bianco, where the chalky minerals have created a waterfall spilling over a white cliff, and where visitors can enjoy the waters for free.

The legendary source of these waters lies to the west, deep in the woods. The **Grotto di San Filippo** is a cave carved into the rock face, in which the 13th-century Saint Filippo built an oratory and hermitage. The story goes that his devotions here resulted in waters springing from the ground, making their way to the nearby town and creating the hot springs there. This ancient site is a silent and magical place, and it's easy to see how stories of miraculous happenings could spring from here.

To the east, across the SR2 highway, a vast valley

is punctuated by a lonely tower atop a distant hill. This is **Radicofani**, whose 1000-year-old fortress is visible for miles in every direction. The town just below the castle is rife with history. The Giardino del Maccione is a wooded World War II memorial garden — the town was, for obvious reasons, an important strategic position during the war. Just below the town is an odd park, the 19th-century Bosco Isabella, where carefully curated trees sit amongst excavations of a pre-Roman dwelling and newer structures like a stone pyramid. Because of the town's altitude in the middle of the low valley, its streets are often foggy at night, creating a magical atmosphere.

A prime lodging in the town is **Casa Holiday del Giardino**, owned by a former mayor of the town. The apartment is ridiculously affordable, considering its position near the top of town and its private garden patio - perfect for enjoying an evening cocktail or meal under the trees.

Farther north, work your way over to the adjacent towns of **Castiglione** and **Rocca d'Orcia**. Both sport castles perched atop rock outcroppings overlooking the Val d'Orcia. The 13th-century **Rocca di Tentennanno** is in better repair and sometimes open for visits. Its crumbling neighbor, the Rocca Aldobrandesca on the adjacent hill, suffers from geological problems as well as having been damaged during WWII. Hidden in the old village below the Tentennano fortress is the restaurant **Cisterna nel Borgo**, which offers a menu combining traditional area dishes with newer internationally-influenced fare.

Proceeding north past these twin castles, along the western edge of the beautiful Val d'Orcia, we come to the ancient spa town of **Bagno Vignoni**, a historic stopping site for pilgrims and travelers; it is a medieval town built around several natural hot springs. In fact, the 16th-century central piazza itself is a steaming pool, fed by one of these springs, creating a unique town square. Others of the springs have been co-opted by hotels and spas, but if you go to the **Parco dei Mulini** nearby, you can take a free swim, while admiring the ancient architecture carved into and built around the volcanic rock. Also worth a visit here is the **Erboristeria Hortus Mirabilis** (Herbalist Shop), a shop that sells soaps, unusual liqueurs, incense, tinctures and creams, the majority of which are locally sourced; and **LibrOrcia**, a little bookstore with a really interesting variety of books. Of particular note is the store's children's section with some striking

Thermal springs of Tuscany

Several towns in Tuscany have the suffix "Terme" after their names; these towns were typically built in ancient times around thermal springs. In many cases, these waters have been co-opted by hotels and resort spas, but a few have free baths out in the open. These locations are notable for their fascinating and unique rock formations made by mineral deposits, as the waters are high in sulfates, bicarbonates, and/or calcium. The hot, pungent mineral waters are purported to carry various healing properties, alleviating ailments from joint pain to digestive problems to skin diseases.

and beautifully illustrated books also suitable for adults. The cookbook section is stocked with books that reveal secrets of this region's cuisine.

Turning east from Bagno Vignoni, head just a bit farther north. Instead of continuing along the SR2 to the medieval walled town of San Quirico d'Orcia (more on this great place farther along), turn east and follow some of the beautiful little roads through the Val d'Orcia to Monticchiello. If you feel like taking a short detour to see Tuscany's most famous hillside road, keep following the SP53. On your way you'll pass the **Quercia delle Checche**, a carefully preserved live oak tree that dates to at least 1650 if not earlier. Named for its placement in the Checche area, it was sometimes called *Quercia delle Streghe* ("witches' oak), being the supposed site of pagan Sabbath ceremonies. Not long past this monument, turn left on SP40. As you wind up through the hills, to your left you'll see the postcard-famous **Strada di Valoresi**. The trees here were planted by the Marchesa Iris Origo, who wrote a remarkable book called "War in Val D'Orcia." It's highly recommend reading either before you travel or while you are there; it's incredible to read about what was happening in 1943-44 to the towns and the people in the area during that time.

After you've taken what you are sure is an award-winning photo of this iconic vista, proceed up the highway and look for the turnoff to Monticchiello. (Note: We don't recommend driving up the Strada di Valoresi itself, as it is a rocky dirt road in poor condition, and it doesn't offer much of a view of anything except pieces of your undercarriage in the rearview mirror.)

A stroll through the tiny medieval hamlet of **Monticchiello** is another of those walks back in time. From the parking lot outside of town, walk up a hill through an olive grove to get to the town gate, Porta di Sant'Agata. During WWII, in April 1944, German soldiers invaded the town in retaliation for a battle that had happened the previous day, in which the Fascists had been forced from the town. The soldiers rounded up all the townspeople on the wall just outside the town gate, with the intention of executing

16

them. They were saved by the intervention of the German wife of one of the townspeople. Look for a modern sculpture just outside the gate, memorializing these events.

Monticchiello also happens to be the home of one of the finest restaurants in Tuscany, **Ristorante Daria**, Make sure to book ahead, as the restaurant is quite small and popular. Daria and her staff serve up traditional Tuscan food with a modern flair; the carefully curated menu changes sea-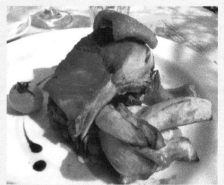sonally. All the pastas here are handmade, and always ask about their various daily specials. Either come here extremely hungry, so you can get all four courses — antipasti, pasta, meat, and dessert — or come back two or three times to have lighter meals and experience more of the menu.

From Monticchiello you can backtrack the way you came, or follow signs to and through Pienza to San Quirico d'Orcia. (Note: The nearly-perfect town of Pienza is San Quirico's smaller, more heavily-visited cousin. We devote much of Itinerary #2 to visiting in and from here.)

Continuing west from San Quirico, we find perched on a hill the town of **Montalcino**, famous for its fine wine Brunello di Montalcino. Wine aficionados will want to make much of visiting Montalcino's many *enoteca* wine bars to sample the local stuff. For us, though, the attraction here is down the hill from the town: The thousand-year-old **Abbazia Sant'Antimo**. Founded as a Benedictine monastery, it is now used by an order of priests from France. The abbey grounds are a great place for a picnic on a nice day. Spend the morning in Montalcino, shopping for a bit of cheese, meat, bread, and some vino (maybe even splurge on a bottle of Brunello?), and then cruise down the hill and enjoy it all in medieval, pastoral style.

A little further to the west down the SP14 is the quaint village of **Sant'Angelo in Colle**. This is Montalcino in miniature: All the same beautiful old buildings, stunning views, and excellent food and wine within a town of a population of dozens,

not thousands. Here, right off of the town square, is **Trattoria Il Pozzo**, an excellent farm-to-table restaurant. They keep a short menu that is determined by what's fresh, local, and seasonal, as well as offering daily specials, which is always a good choice in a place like this. The restaurant is connected to one of the local wineries; this, combined with its position in the heart of Brunello country (one of the most famous wine regions in the world), assures a wide selection of great wines at a decent price.

Now we come back around at last to **San Quirico d'Orcia**. The name of the town is in honor of Saint Quiricus, a semi-mythical child martyr on whom a great many cults have been founded throughout Europe (and after whom many towns are named, hence the "d'Orcia" appended to this particular San Quirico). This is a well-preserved medieval walled town that has limitless charms and little-known architectural interests. A day or three can easily be spent just wandering the streets and the beautiful, extensive (and free) town garden grounds, **Horti Leoni**.

Try visiting its several churches, such as the large **Collegiate Church of Saints Quiricus & Julietta**, and the much smaller but atmospheric **Church of Santa Maria Assunta** at the other end of town. On the main square, Piazza della Libertà, is the **Church of San Francesco** (a.k.a. Church of Santa Maria of Vitaleta). This church gets its "alias" by virtue of housing a famous (perhaps infamous) clay statue of the Madonna. The statue, by 16th-century artist Andrea della Robbia, used to be housed in the Chapel of Vitaleta, an iconic building that sits on a hill in the countryside between Pienza and San Quirico (see Itinerary #2). Ownership of the statue was a point of much contention between the two

towns centuries ago; evidently San Quirico ultimately made Pienza an offer they couldn't refuse.

All of the architecture in this town gives the impression that you've stepped back in time some 700 years. Night-time here is magical: Our own footsteps on the ancient cobbles, dishes clinking in houses after dinner, and an occasional fluttering flock of swifts are the only sounds we hear as we walk through nearly deserted side streets. For two people from Philadelphia and New York, the idea of walking through a deserted part of a city at night could have seemed scary. But with an almost nonexistent crime rate, our greatest fear was not having room for one more dessert at the cafe before going to bed.

San Quirico offers modern shopping as well. **Erbario Toscano** sells soaps, perfumes, reed diffusers, candles, and hand wipes, among other things, all made in Tuscany. Our favorites are the soaps made from black pepper and olive oil. Beer fans will be happy to discover the **Birrificio San Quirico**, an on-site brewery and shop whose artisan ales are highly prized in the region.

For coffee or *vino* and a bite to eat, drop in at the bar **Angolo del Vino**. Take a seat in the small back garden, but watch out for the pet turtles ("*tartaruga*") who wander freely there. Also note the giant rosemary tree framing the outside garden door.

Dining well in San Quirico is easy — the only problem is having too few meal-times to try every

place. Don't miss **Osteria Cardinale** (near the Collegiata) where the hosts gregariously serve up wonderful traditional plates, including a great *tagliata di manzo* (sliced beef). You may also enjoy the romantically candle-lit **Trattoria Osenna**, which offers house-made sausage and locally-sourced meats. Try the *stinco di maiale*, a bacon-wrapped leg of pork that looks like something Fred Flinstone would eat. On cold nights, take advantage of the open fire at **Trattoria al Vecchio Forno**, where they serve three house-made *liquori* of cinnamon, *liquorizia* (anise), and saffron.

The roadways in this section of Tuscany wind through some of the most beautiful and picturesque landscape anywhere. It is a good idea to allow a lot more time than seems necessary, as you'll want to stop and take pictures, or simply to let the countryside soak into your psyche. You can spend hours just sitting on the side of the road, watching storms roll over the hills, listening to birds and cowbells, or waiting on the light to reveal those magical moments. Phrases like "it's the journey not the destination that's important" were invented for places like this, so enjoy the drive.

Piancastagnaio

Ristorante Anna

Must have reservations for Sunday lunch, always served family style. In a residential neighborhood, outside the town wall. Never miss a chance to eat their mushroom and chestnut soup, or any of their paper-thin ravioli. There are also rooms here, starting at 90€.

Closed Sunday night and Monday.
http://www.annaristorante.com

Santa Fiora

Ristorante Il Barilotto

On a side street near the main square. Small family run restaurant, feels like you're eating in a treasured family home. Be sure to ask what is fresh, there are daily specials and those are the ones you'll want to stick to.

Open every day for lunch and dinner.
https://ilbarilotto.business.site/

San Quirico d'Orcia

Osteria del Cardinale

On the main street in town, near the top of the hill. Two large dining rooms, but still a good idea to book on weekends in high season. Husband and wife Anastasio and Luigina run the place, he handles the front of house and she is the chef.

Closed Mondays.
http://www.osteriadelcardinale.it/

Trattoria Osenna

On the main street, near the entrance at the bottom of the hill. Real candles on the tables and in the lanterns outside create a romantic environment. For tastes from their wood ovens, try bruschette with melted pecorino or roast meats.

Closed Wednesdays.

http://www.trattoriaosenna.com

Trattoria al Vecchio Forno

Popular restaurant in town, reservations recommended. Inviting atmosphere, in winters there is an open fire, and they have some delicious house made liqueurs — don't miss the saffron one.

Open every day.

Monticchiello

Ristorante Daria

Stylish, newly remodeled restaurant owned by locally famous restauranteur Daria Cappelli. Menu changes seasonally and items are locally sourced; many of those sources are listed on the menu.

Closed Wednesday.

https://www.ristorantedaria.it

Sant'Angelo in Colle

Trattoria il Pozzo

Fantastic restaurant in a tiny town that reminds us of what Montalcino must have looked like 40 years ago. Excellent food in a completely untouristed town. That said, make reservations as this place is extremely popular with Italians.

Closed Tuesdays. In low season, they may be closed if they have no reservations.

http://www.trattoriailpozzo.com/

Rocca d'Orcia

Cisterna nel Borgo

The only restaurant in this tiny little borgo, Cisterna offers traditional Tuscan fare alongside quirky treats invented by the creative chef. Be sure to leave room for one of their gorgeous and unique desserts.

Open dinner Tuesday-Sunday; lunch also Saturday and Sunday. Closed Mondays.

https://www.cisternanelborgo.com/

Viva d'Orcia

Taverna Pian Delle Mura

A "Slow Food" restaurant; everything here is handmade, seasonal, and sourced locally. The last page or two of the menu is an extensive list of local farmers, butchers, and vendors who provide the ingredients. Though this restaurant is well off the beaten path, a reservation is a must here as this is a very popular place with food-loving locals.

Open dinner Tuesday-Sunday, lunch also Saturday and Sunday. Closed Mondays.

http://www.tavernapiandellemura.it/

Pitigliano

Hostaria del Ceccottino

Located in Piazza san Gregorio in this town known as "Little Jerusalem", Ceccottino offers traditional dishes of the region, including Tuscan Jewish fare. For those wishing to explore the town more deeply, Ceccottino offers a few B&B rooms.

Closed Thursdays.

https://ceccottino.com/

Bagno Vignoni

Locanda del Loggiato

Absolutely beautiful B&B in one of our favorite, most romantic "hidden" towns. Day trippers evacuate at night, so we like to stay here and enjoy the quiet atmosphere one they've gone. A common rooms for guests boasts a grand piano and tons of books. Unlike many B&Bs, this one offers an elaborate breakfast.

Rooms from 90€.

Radicofani

Casa Holiday del Giardino

Just a few minutes' walk from Radicofani's landmark castle tower, this AirBnB rental is owned by Anna, a former Mayor of Radicofani. It's a small house, with two bedrooms and a private garden. Anna is a gracious host and Radicofani is a gorgeous away-from-it-all hill town.

From 67€/night.

Note: Hostaria del Ceccottino, Ristorante Anna, and Cisterna nel Borgo from our "Where to Eat section also offer a few B&B rooms.

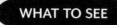

WHAT TO SEE

Pitigliano

Synagogue and Museo Ebraico

From April to October from 10am to 1pm and from 2.30pm to 6pm, From November to March from 10am to 12.30pm and from 3pm to 5pm

Closed: Saturday and Jewish holidays

www.lapiccolagerusalemme.it

Montalcino

Abbey of Sant'Antimo

This ancient Abbey was founded in the 9th century; the present Abbey dates to the 12thC. The Abbey is open year round but opening times vary according to season so check the website. This is still an active place of worship so please don't visit during Mass unless you are there for that purpose. Self-guided video tours are available for a small fee. At the monastic pharmacy here you can buy products made by the monks. Those looking for a spiritual retreat can also arrange to stay in the guesthouse.

http://www.antimo.it

WHERE TO SHOP

Santa Fiora

Queste Terre Alimenti Tipici

This small little shop is right on the main square. Beans, farro, local wine and liqueurs, hand made soaps, salts, honeys, and sauces, all locally made and sourced. Samples of liqueurs available.

Closed Monday. Open 9-1 and 4:30-7:30; Sundays open 9-1.

San Quirico d'Orcia

Birrificio San Quirico

Pop in and have a cold one, watch them making beer in the brewing vats in the back room, and take a few home with you as a gift. Beer jam and other products on sale here as well.

http://birrificiosanquirico.it/

Bagno Vignoni

Librorcia

A cute bookstore run by Simone Gallerani, who speaks perfect English, and can help you choose from the diverse and interesting titles here. Unusual, hard-to-find books, beautiful children's books fitting as gifts for adults, great cookbooks, large English language section. Art displayed on walls by local artists available for sale.

http://www.librorcia.com

Erboristeria Hortus Mirabilis

Small shop carrying liqueurs, soaps, teas, tinctures, creams, candles and more, all locally made. Hard-to-find, small batch items.

Open every day 10:30-1 and 3-7:30; open 30 minutes earlier on weekends

http://www.hortusmirabilis.it/

Abbadia San Salvatore

Aurelia Visconti

Located in an office park outside the center of town you'll find this wonderful little liquorificio (liqueur maker). You'll find their liqueurs at several local restaurants, including our favorite, Ristorante Anna. Many are made using the ancient recipes of the monks of San Salvatore's abbey. They also make sauces for meat and game, jams, and salsas. An unmissable place for the food lover. Hours vary so call ahead to make sure they're open and bring cash.

http://www.aureliovisconti.com/

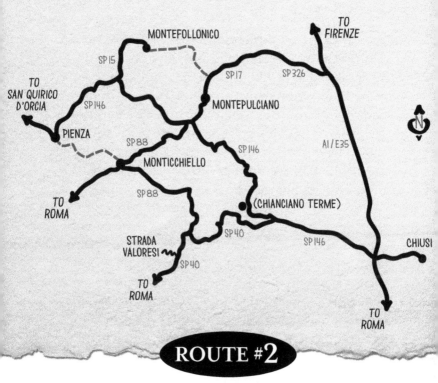

ROUTE #2

Southern Tuscany
Around Pienza

Tuscany has hundreds of small, beautiful, ancient hill towns, all overlooking some stunning vista and looking like the set of a medieval costume drama.

Pienza is the quintessential example of these. A UNESCO World Heritage Site, Pienza started as a small village called Corsignano. Silvio Piccolomini, better known as Pope Pius II was born here and redesigned the town in the mid-15th century. The **Palazzo Piccolomini** remains one of the town's large attractions along with the Duomo (cathedral), which Pius commissioned and consecrated. It dominates Pienza's skyline as it looks out over the Val d'Orcia. Pius designed the cathedral to overhang the hillside cliff, to make it distinct and imposing from afar. Because of this, the aspe (the altar area and beyond) has been sinking for centuries. More on this in a moment.

Upon entering the town walls, a distinctive scent wafts through the air. Pienza is famous for its **Pecorino di Pienza**, a sheeps' cheese particular to this area. Many stores in town partner with

farmers and sell the delicious stuff, and the resulting aroma seems to emanate from the very walls
all over town.

Pecorino di Pienza

Another iconic Tuscan food is *pecorino*, a cheese made from
sheep's milk. The pecorino of the town of Pienza is regarded as
the best of Tuscany, made exclusively from a specific local breed
of sheep and with traditional methods that have been passed
down through millennia. Some pecorino is *fresco*, soft and
creamy after aging for a mere 1-2 months; others are *stagionato*,
seasoned with various coverings (dried peppers or rosemary ash
or leaves from nut-trees, to name just a few varieties) and aged
in caves or cellars for as long as a year and a half.

It is a perfect, medieval walled hill-town; as
such, many tourists have beaten a track to its gates
searching for "off-the-beaten track" destinations.
We recommend visiting Pienza in the off-season,
but even in peak months beat the crowds and get
the most out of town by staying for a few days or
even a week. It is a perfect base for exploring
southern Tuscany. Enjoy day trips to other (even
smaller) towns and return in the cool of the
evening when most of the Pienza day-trippers
have boarded their bus back to Firenze.

Pienza is close to San Quirico and to Monticchiello and its great restaurant **Ristorante Daria**
(see Itinerary 1). The 10 km drive west to San

Quirico is one of the most beautiful stretches of roadway on the planet. Look to the south as you head west, for a little chapel across the farmlands on the next ridge. This is the postcard-famous **Capella di Vitaleta**, and it's another chance for a prize-worthy photo.

Drive about 35 km in the other direction to visit **Chiusi**, which was a capital city of the Etruscans, founded around the 7th century BC. The remains of the Etruscan culture, which pre-dates the Roman Empire by centuries, are found all over Italy. Chiusi's **Museo Archeologico Nazionale** is home to one of the biggest collections of tombs and other artifacts of this once thriving civiliza-

tion. Also of great interest in this small town is the **Labyrinth of Porsenna**, a series of ancient underground tunnels built by the Etruscans. Visitors can walk through these by visiting the Cathedral, which also features a tower with commanding views of the countryside.

While you're in Chiusi, consider lunch at **Osteria La Solita Zuppa**, a favorite of the locals. Soup (*zuppa*) is their specialty. Several selections vary seasonally, plus the homemade pastas and wood-fired pizzas gives the place a cozy, woodsy scent.

With dessert, try the tasty homemade cinnamon liqueur. And don't miss the post-meal coffee service. It's presented in a style so elaborate and charming, it must be seen to be believed.

Nearby **Montepulciano** is a large town by our standards, and it is well-covered in countless guidebooks; we only make two outstanding suggestions here. In the *centro*, chefs and other kitchen connoisseurs will want to visit the **Bottega del Rame**, the shop of 3rd-generation copper artisan Cesare Mazzetti. On the hill at the edge of town sits the famous Chiesa di San Biagio. Directly next to this is the equally beautiful **Ristorante La Grotta**, where diners can enjoy seasonal and fresh dishes while overlooking the church.

About 10 km to the north of Pienza sits the far quieter village of **Montefollonico**. From this charming walled town you can overlook the larger towns of Pienza and Montepulciano and the valleys between. Our favorite restaurant here is **13 Gobbi** found just inside the town gate. Proprietors Albo and Simonetta serve up delicious, traditional Tuscan fare. Try their signature dish, *tagliatelle in formo di pecorino* — warm, house made pasta dredged around inside the hollowed-out shell of a *pecorino* cheese wheel, then sprinkled with white pepper before serving. Albo, an outgoing, funny guy, brings the *pecorino* shell on its own little table to make a show of it. It's delicious AND entertaining.

After lunch, walk off some of that *pecorino* strolling through the town's few blocks and taking in views and historic architecture, including an ancient church down a little path just outside the walls. After a dozen visits to this town over the years, we've never found this church to be open for visitors, but the walk is gorgeous nevertheless.

A handful of other towns sit within an easy drive of Pienza, some of which are detailed in Itinerary #3, but Pienza is a fantastic destination in itself. You could easily stay there for days without quite feeling like you've seen it all.

We recommend three different lodging options in Pienza, Just inside the town wall, **Il Giardino Segreto** (meaning "secret garden") has modest but immaculate rooms and a private garden, inviting in any season. As a temporary escape from the crowds, occasionally we'll grab some food from one of the local stores (cheese, fruit, bread, a few slices of *salumi*, maybe some chocolate or *biscotti*) and enjoy it with a bottle of wine or *prosecco* in walled seclusion. Each room has a mini-fridge, so you can plan ahead and chill your bottle in advance.

Just outside the town wall, try **B&B Camere Andrei**, a very comfortable place with a nice breakfast offering and that most valuable of tourist-town amenities: Free parking. Some of the rooms also have little balconies, perfect for enjoying wine and a sunset.

Hidden just inside the wall in this corner the popular **Buon Gusto Gelateria** serves artisanal gelato and fresh-squeezed juices in creative flavors, using items in the cold case on display at the front of the shop.

Guests of the little B&B **La Chiocarella** can duck down the tiny *vicolo* ("alley") by the same name to escape the crowds in the lodging's private garden. The rooms are small but perfect, and the large continental breakfast includes goodies from local bakers.

While in Pienza explore its **Duomo** (cathedral). It's free to enjoy the artwork and architecture. Exit the church and hug its right-hand wall to the entrance of the **Baptistery**, predictably named after San Giovanni (Saint John). On display here are a dozen or so large pages of medieval music notation (called tablature) with very intricate and colorful designs outlining the margins, containing hidden birds, faces and hands. Better yet, on the far side of

the baptistery is an entrance to a series of lower catacombs. These are fascinating to explore: They were modernized and solidified in the early 20th century when support construction became necessary as the entire church began to sag under its own weight on the clay cliffs of the hillside. Walking through these tunnels, you feel like you are in some secret part of the city. You can follow the tunnels to their ends, which have barred wooden doors. Peek through the cracks — you'll see the roads that ring Pienza. As you take a walk around town on those roads, you'll know where those secret doors go.

The best attraction here is also free: **Pienza's "balcony,"** the rampart that extends along the south side of the town. The panorama of the Val d'Orcia with Monte Amiata in the distance is a breathtaking view,

especially at sunrise or sunset. For an even nicer (and quieter) walk with the same view, exit the west gate and pass the little park. Look for signs leading to the "Passegiata" — this is the Via Santa Caterina, which becomes a gravel and dirt path that runs along the edge of the cliff. We like to bring a hunk of *pecorino*, a piece of fruit and a bottle of chilled *prosecco*, and watch the sunset from one of the many stone benches on this "balcony." Further down the walk is the centuries-old Chiesa di Santa Caterina, with a double belfry. Just down the hill from here is the 11th-century **Pieve di Corsignano**, where Pope Pius II was baptized. The church is evocative and interesting— note its atypically circular bell tower, and the fantastical carvings over the exterior doorways. These depict many Biblical scenes like the Nativity, but they also include animals and mythological creatures.

Being a food-lover in Pienza is like being a kid in a candy store. (Oh, and they do have a candy store.) Our

favorite is **Trattoria da Fiorella**, run by two brothers and their mother. It's right next door to Il Giardino Segreto. One of their occasional specialties is a *sformato di pecorino* (sort of a little cheese soufflé), dressed with different seasonal fare. Their pasta is handmade, like the chewy *pici* (a regional specialty, a hand rolled, long noodle). The *secondi* (second course, meat dishes), which we often skip elsewhere, are excellent, especially the roast pork with mushrooms in pastry. We like to reserve one of their upstairs tables, to overlook our fellow diners. This is a popular and small place, so stop in at lunchtime or the night before to reserve your dinner table.

Pienza offers other excellent dining options. **Baccus L'Osteria** serves a delicious *antipasti* plate for two with local cheeses, salumi, olives, and honey. A popular *secondi* is a sliced beef filet with a balsamic reduction. Their whipped mascarpone dessert with seasonal toppings  is another specialty. **Latte di Luna** and **Trattoria La Buca delle Fate** are both casual and frequented by many locals; Latte di Luna used to (and maybe still does) have a talking Myna bird who greets you from his cage at the door — in Italian of course. La Buca delle Fate serves a baked *pecorino* cheese in a clay pot, to be eaten with their crusty bread. And of course there are many bars in town, a couple of which are on the wall walk. At **Bar Piccolomini**, you can enjoy a quick bite of their house-made food along with your coffee or *vino*.

Pane Toscano — salt-free bread

Every meal in Tuscany begins with a basket of traditional *pane Toscano*, made without salt and therefore quite bland. Some sources attribute this lack to an ancient tax on salt, which made the Tuscans learn to do without; others suggest that the forces of Pisa, at war with Florence in the Middle Ages, placed a blockade on the salt shipments to the interior, forcing the Tuscans to make unsalted bread. Either way, the result is a perfect vehicle for mopping up delicious olive oil or the end of your pasta sauce, a practice known as *"fare la scarpetta"*, literally "to make the little shoe".

Pienza also has a few artisans not to be missed: The **Bottega Artigiana del Cuoio** is a tiny shop on the main street where leather craftsman Valerio Trufelli makes purses, bags, books, wallets, belts, and many other items by hand, which he stamps with his own personal logo. (If you missed it, we relate a wonderful anecdote about Valerio in the introduction chapter.)

We return again and again to visit **Ceramiche L'arte Linda Bai**, a ceramic gallery. Linda's work is

beautiful — she crafts and then paints everything by hand — and we have brought home many of her pieces over the years. (We even commissioned a piece for a very reasonable price.) The gallery opens up in the rear to an ancient Etruscan-era cave dug into the stone of the hillside, so visiting the place is as much an exploration of pre-history as well as of local artistry.

Pienza hosts a cheese festival, showcasing its famous *pecorino*, on the first Sunday of September; and it holds a flower festival in May. Its market day is Friday. This town is worth visiting anytime of the year, any day of the week; but the best way to experience it is to stay a few days, become immersed in village life, and explore the surrounding countryside from there.

WHERE TO STAY

Pienza

Il Giardino Segreto

Just inside the town wall, Giardino Segreto offers both rooms and small apartments. There is no parking (you must find it in town, which is easy in off-season), but the great perk here is the garden, a walled-off respite from the 'city'. Each room has a coffee service and a mini fridge so it's easy to chill a bottle of prosecco to enjoy in the afternoons.

Double rooms from 75€.

http://www.ilgiardinosegretopienza.it

B&B Camere Andrei

Just outside the town wall, Camere Andrei offers clean, comfortable rooms, each with a large bathroom. Some rooms have a small balcony as well, and a mini fridge. Free parking on site, an unusual perk. Standard breakfast offerings available in the morning in the communal room.

Double rooms from 68€.

http://www.camereandrei.it

La Chiocarella

Beautiful rooms in a B&B in the center of town. There is a private garden here for guests to enjoy, and the breakfast laid out every morning is one of the most extensive we've ever seen. Owner Roberta is a kind and gracious host who makes you feel at home right away.

Double rooms from 90€.

http://www.portalepienza.it/chiocarella.htm

WHERE TO EAT

Chiusi

Osteria La Solita Zuppa

Cute little Osteria in the hill town of Chiusi, specializing in soup. If it's in season, try the artichoke and mint, and for dessert, the house made cinnamon liqueur.

Closed Tuesdays.

http://www.lasolitazuppa.it

Montefollonico

13 Gobbi

Charming restaurant in the tiny town of Montefollonico. Simonetta runs the kitchen and her gregarious husband Albo runs the front of house. Try the special of the house: Tagliatelle in forma di pecorino — a delicious dish that comes with its own show.

Closed January.

http://www.montefollonico.it/13gobbi.php

Pienza

Trattoria da Fiorella

One of our favorite restaurants, we never miss eating here when we're in Pienza or anywhere nearby. Incredible food, inviting atmosphere, if you stay in Pienza a few days you'll want to book in at this Trattoria more than once to experience much of the menu.

Closed Wednesday and two weeks in July.

http://www.trattoriadafiorella.it/

Baccus L'Osteria

Sweet little Osteria located right on Corso Rosselino. Romantic atmosphere, candlelight, walls stacked with cooking objects, art and books. Best to make a reservation, especially in the summer months. Ask for the romantic little booth table, which is just inside the front door to the right. Don't miss the mascarpone cream for dessert.

Closed Thursdays.

http://www.baccusosteria.it/

Latte di Luna

Popular with locals and tourists, Latte di Luna can be found at the east end of town. A casual environment here, affordable, no-fuss food. If you're lucky you'll get there at a time of year when they still have their own house-made herbal amaro.

Closed Tuesdays.

http://www.portalepienza.it/latteluna.htm

Trattoria La Buca delle Fate

A favorite with locals, this large restaurant is found on Corso Rosselino. Try the 'pecorino in forno' (basically a big dish of melted pecorino served with crusty bread), and the house made desserts.

Closed Mondays.

http://www.ristorantelabucadellefatepienza.it/

Buon Gusto Gelateria

Tucked away on a small side street, you'll be able to easily find this gelato shop by looking for the ever-present line. It's worth the wait! The gelato is hand made here and the flavors are inventive. A cold case in the front is stocked with fresh fruits and veg used in the gelato, and also in smoothies they make to order.

Open every day 11am-8pm.

https://www.facebook.com/BuonGustoGelateriaPienza/

Montepulciano

Ristorante La Grotta

La Grotta has it all: Excellent food, stunning views, great service, beautiful atmosphere. Traditional Tuscan cuisine served with a modern twist. Excellent service in a gorgeous setting away from the crowds.

Closed Wednesdays and early January - mid March.

http://www.lagrottamontepulciano.it/

WHERE TO SHOP

Pienza

Bottega Artigiana del Cuoio

Tiny artisanal leather shop on the main street of Pienza, one of our favorites. Owner and artisan Valerio Truffelli hand makes everything in the shop, and will accept commissions as well.

Corso Rossellino 58

Ceramiche L'arte Linda Bai

We've been to Linda's shop so many times we consider her a friend. Her gorgeous ceramic works include plates, bowls, tiles, clocks and cups of every size. She will also accept commissions for individual pieces of art. All pieces are created and hand painted in the shop. Prices range from very, very affordable

to very expensive depending on size and technique required.
Via Gozzante 33
http://www.ceramichebai.it

Montepulciano

Bottega del Rame (Copper Shop)

Cesare Mazzetti is a third generation copper artisan whose shop is a treasure trove of handmade copper pans, distilleries, plates, and more. Next door is a small copper museum as well. Via dell'Opio nell Corso, 64. Open every day 10am-7pm. Holidays vary.
www.rameria.com

WHAT TO SEE

Chiusi

Museo Archeologico Nazionale

Etruscan museum in center of town, housing many artifacts found in nearby tombs. If you have time and inclination let them know when you buy a ticket that you want a tour of the tombs; the Tomba della Pellegrina is free and open usually every day; the Tomba della Scimmia is only open Wednesdays, Thursdays and Saturdays and costs an additional 3€. Guides are friendly and well informed and the tombs make a memorable visit.

Museum entrance 6€, free for children under 18

and half price ages 19-25. Open every day from 9am-8pm, last entrance at 7:30pm. Check out the new "Chiusi Card" that gets you in to all museums for 10€.

http://www.archeotoscana.beniculturali.it/index.php?it/147/chiusi-museo-archeologico-nazionale

Labyrinth of Porsenna

The Labyrinth is a series of ancient tunnels underneath Chiusi's cathedral. Guided tours take you through the tunnels and in to a large chamber, all several hundred feet underground. Not for the faint of heart or the claustrophobic, but everyone else will not want to miss this unique experience.

Tickets 6€, but for 10€ there is a new "Chiusi Card" that will grant you access to all town museums.

http://www.prolocochiusi.it

Pienza

Baptistery (Lower Church of St. John the Baptist)

Just round the corner from the Duomo, this museum houses some great art pieces, including some medieval tablature that will be interesting to anyone who likes music. The catacombs are well worth a visit as well, and have descriptions and photos posted throughout.

Entry is 2€.

Pieve di Corsignano

Oldest church in Pienza, just a 15 minute walk downhill from the center center of town. Open by appointment or on Fridays, but worth it to see from the outside only.

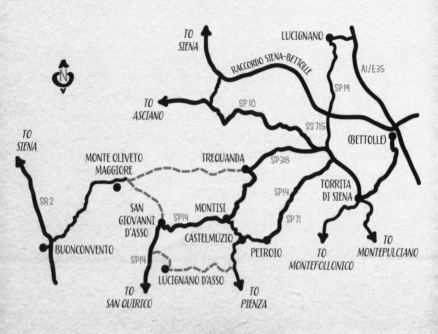

ROUTE #3

Southern Tuscany
The Crete Senesi

*Between the Val d'Orcia to the south and the town of
Siena to the north lies a distinctly beautiful region.
Similar to the Val d'Orcia, with winding hillside roads
and tall cypress trees outlining cultivated farms and
pastures, the landscape is frequently punctuated by
unusual clay geology.*

Barren gray peaks jut out of the rolling terrain, evoking a lunar landscape. This distinctive Sienese clay ("*Crete Senesi*"), fortifies some of Tuscany's best food, including wine, olive oil, truffles, and the adorable but regrettably delicious *cinta senese* pigs. These hogs sport a belt ("*cinta*") of white around the middle of their black coats, and their meat is used frequently in regional food .

We focus our visit to this region on two re-remarkable places: The tiny and charming town of **Trequanda**, home to one of our favorite restaurants in the world; and the 14th century Benedic-tine Abbey of Monte Oliveto Maggiore, an oft-overlooked but truly incredible historic site. Between these two locations are dozens of little villages and points of interest that make for an enchanting several days of driving, eating, and enjoying Tuscan life.

Trequanda is a beautiful unassuming medieval town, sitting above rolling hillsides covered in olive groves and vineyards. Some of Tuscany's best food-stuffs, especially the olive oil, are produced here. The small gothic church, **Santi Pietro e Andrea**, on the tiny main Piazza Garibaldi, boasts a striking Sienese checkerboard facade, made with alternating light and dark bricks. Get there at the right time of day and you'll hear the town's matrons inside, intoning their call-and-response prayers.

A small park just outside the piazza offers a pleasant place to sit with a *gelato*, or to wait in cool tranquility for your table reservation at **Il Conte Matto.** The restaurant's name means "Crazy Count", derived from the medieval townspeople's viewpoint that the ruling Cacciaconti family of the 11th-13th centuries were insane. Today this is one of the region's finest restaurants, serving a mix of traditional fare and a few modern dishes. It is a perfect mix of fine food (complete with white tablecloths and wine buckets) and a relaxed, casual atmosphere.

On our website we write extensively and superlatively of the restaurant's many culinary virtues, but here are a few essential points: The patio offers a picturesque setting for enjoying a meal . We like to stoke our appetites with a couple of glasses (or a bottle) of their refreshing, sparkling white wine, made just down the hill. Savor this with a bit of bread dipped in their olive oil (but DON'T fill up!). While every dish is a delight — proprietor Davide has been courted by top restaurants in Rome and elsewhere — our favorite is the simple but delicious *pici alla briciole. Pici* is a thick hand-rolled pasta, typical of Tuscany. Here it's topped with crunchy, olive-oily breadcrumbs (*briciole*). It sounds strange, but it's the best way to appreciate this great oil.

The olive oil served and sold at Conte Matto ranks among the world's best. Also made just

down the hill at a nearby farm, this oil is used in fine restaurants all over Europe, including Gerard Depardieu's establishment in Paris. Many people come to this restaurant, buy an entire bottle to taste at their table, and take the rest home. If they aren't sold out, which often happens in early autumn, we buy 2-3 bottles before we leave.

Olive oil

Nearly every region of Italy claims to be a source of excellent olive oil, and Tuscany is no exception. The region's rocky ground is well-suited to growing olives and grapes, and little else, so olive oil production has been key to prosperity here for centuries. In autumn, the *raccolta* (harvest) is a most important event, and in some towns, whole neighborhoods turn out to the groves to pick the olives at just the right time. A good fresh olive oil on a plate with a little salt and a loaf of *pane Toscano* is as close to a perfect food as we can imagine.

Conte Matto has a few rooms available, and we highly recommend taking one for a couple of nights. There's nothing like having a hours-long, epic meal and then just rolling up the stairs to a four-poster bed with a view of the vineyards and olive groves just outside the castle window.

Before heading south into the heart of the Crete Senesi, consider taking a little excursion 20 km north of Trequanda to **Lucignano**, close to the Al autostrada. Not to be confused with Lucignano d'Asso, further south, the town of Lucignano is a well-preserved medieval hill town. Like many towns in strategic positions, this one was heavily fought over for centuries and variously claimed by Siena, Perugia, Arezzo, and Firenze. The main point of interest is the design of the town itself. The streets are laid out in concentric ellipses, each interior one higher up than the one surrounding it, just like a tiered cake. The top part is the oldest, with the fortress dating to the 13th century.

We recommend the charming **B&B Cappuccini** in Lucignano. Just a few blocks outside the town wall in a cozy little house, owner Lucia Bianchini graciously offers three apartments to rent. It's an easy walk up into the town to dine and explore the rings of streets and their shops, restaurants, and ancient architecture.

Another lodging we love, **Hotel Gianduia**, hides behind a little door on the street that circles the old town. Its gorgeous rooms all have vaulted ceilings painted with frescoes from the 19th century,

and the building boasts a large patio overlooking the Tuscan hills, perfect for enjoying a glass of wine. Next door to the hotel is **Zenzero**, a restaurant with a unique concept. Three fixed menus - "red" for meat dishes, "green" for vegetarian, and "blue" for seafood-based plates — offer three types of fine dining experiences. We took the time to try them all, and they were all were first-rate, imaginative and delicious.

For a very upscale dining experience, try lunch at the remote and magical **Castello di Modanella**, to the west of Lucignano. The food was outstanding — a deliciously creamy chickpea soup, decadent wine-soaked ribs — and the service impeccable. This is a much fancier place than we usually visit, but now and then a special occasion calls for a bit of indulgence.

Alternatively, if you're in the area in March, check out the *Palio dei Somari* in **Torrita di Siena**. This is a race modeled on the famous Palio of Siena, but instead of horses, the riders from Torrita's different *contrade* (neighborhoods) are riding *somari* - donkeys. The animals are as uncooperative as one might expect, as they amble around the short track. The whole town shuts down for an all-day celebration for the event, including parades of the town's *contrade* with medieval costumes, trumpets and drums.

Driving south from Tre-
quanda on SP38, we en-
counter a trio of adorable
hilltop villages. Miniscule
Montisi is home to **Ristorante
Da Roberto**, one of those
places with only a single
hand-written menu on a
chalkboard. This is a good sign
(literally and figuratively), as it means that each
dish is thought out and made each day. Everything
is local, organic, and beautifully prepared, de-
pendent on what's fresh in Montisi's market or in
the other nearby towns. A bit further south we
come to the walled village of **Castelmuzio**. Visitors
can walk the entirety of this medieval town in
minutes, though it's worthwhile to take much
more time to enjoy the town's ancient charm.

A lovely restaurant and lodging, **Locanda
Casalmustia**, sits in the very center of town underneath the church's bell tower. Or, if you're in the
mood for a more casual setting for a quick snack,
the town has a little "balcony" with a few benches,
facing south and overlooking much of the
Val d'Orcia, including Pienza and Monte Amiata.
Grab a bottle of wine and a hunk of *pecorino* at the
town's Co-op grocery (just down the steps from
this overlook) and savor the tastes and the views
of this timeless place.

To the east is another hilltop village, **Petroio**. Driving through the town *centro* is for advanced drivers only (and only with compact cars), given the VERY narrow streets. Driving it requires paying close attention to the *senso unico* (one-way) signs, and pulling in the side mirrors. Avoid that adventure by parking in the large lot on the north side of the town, and walking up a steep but well-made pathway to the village. Either way it's worth it to stop for a drink or a meal on the flower-filled hilltop patio of the upscale **Palazzo Brandano** hotel.

Backtracking to the initial route, continue on to **San Giovanni d'Asso**, to find the unusual **Bosco della Ragnaia**, just a little further north of the *centro*. Though it looks like some Renaissance garden laid out in the woods, it was created by the eccentric American artist Sheppard Craige in 1996. Admission is free, and the scenery priceless.

On the road south toward Torrenieri, take a hard-to-find turn east (about 3 km south from San Giovanni d'Asso), up a dirt track to the tiny medieval hamlet of **Lucignano d'Asso**. Don't miss the adorable bar/restaurant/market with its entrance framed with vines covered in thousands of flowers. In addition to local meats and cheeses (they make a great sandwich!), they sell glasses of local *liquori*, like the monk-crafted *Flora di Monteoliveto*. Bottles can be purchased at the monastery a few stops later. At the back of the shop is a little cave dating to Etruscan times, where they incongruously store bottled water and Coke.

Lucignano d'Asso also has an oil vendor on the same road (there is in fact only one road), as it is the base of one of the olive groves that we've just driven through. They're open infrequently, but their oil is sold at the bar; do yourself a favor and bring a bottle of this stuff home. Oh, and as you're driving through here, watch out for the free-roaming peacock.

Retracing again to the main route, proceed

through Torrenieri to the SR2 highway and turn north to reach **Buonconvento**. For a truly off-the-beaten-track experience, wind your way west past Buonconvento up to **Murlo**. A tiny, medieval walled hill town (its castle was built sometime in the 12th century), Murlo has an interesting distinction: Researchers recently discovered that the modern residents of this historically isolated town share a great deal of DNA with that of the ancient Etruscans, and they are proud of their heritage. The centerpiece of the old town is its Etruscan Museum and Antiquarium.

By far the biggest town on this itinerary, Buonconvento is still a small town — an old medieval walled city surrounded by a bit of modern-day sprawl. As this is not a hill town, it's accessible town for everyone, quite flat and easily walkable. Parking can be found on the street, or in the big lot on the east side of the town, just outside the wall.

Buonconvento has a few notable places, including the town garden just inside the wall and the 14th century **Church of Saints Peter and Paul**. Notable for a "Madonna with Child" by 15th century artist Matteo di Giovanni, whose work also can be seen in the nearby **Museum of Sacred Art**, the church also flaunts a modern stained glass depiction of the crucifixion that anachronistically includes Gandhi, MLK, and JFK.

If you're looking for a memorable gift, stop by the knitting shop, **Susy.** Over the years we have brought back several items from this shop owned by Susanna Gorelli. She sells bags, jackets and dresses, but the real treasures are her gorgeous hand-knit items. Scarves come in every variety, plus gloves, hats and sweaters, all handmade by the women who work here. Look for the "Susy" label for a particularly distinctive tube-like scarf that is thin and delicate, like a spider web, but warmer.

For lunch, grab a table at the casual family-run restaurant **Da Mario**. Bottles of wine sit on the tables, and you pay for what you drink. There are no menus — they just tell you what's available that day. In these situations, it's best to ask what's handmade and in-house. Typically they serve a couple of pasta options and a couple of different sauces, all traditional. Two or three meat dishes round out the offerings. Don't miss the roasted turkey in a creamy gorgonzola sauce if it's in the rotation. Locals fill up this place, so it's best to stop by in the morning and ask for a table in the afternoon, and then use the time in between to explore town.

Alternatively, try **La Porta di Sotto** for a more modern take on Tuscan cuisine. The servers here will be happy to help you select a bottle from their extensive and carefully-curated wine list.

For a much more informal but utterly memorable lunchtime experience, go to the **Consorzio Agrario di Siena di Giovanni Bizzarro**, on the north side of town across the street from the parking lot. The store stocks various high-quality local products in addition to making some of their own dishes in the deli. On Thursdays be sure to get a few slices (*fette*) of their roast *porchetta*, which is salty and delicious, and good to eat even cold. We like to buy all manner of local goodies — wine, cheese, a couple of meats, salad fixings, oil, fruit — and drive northeast up the highway (SP451) following signs to Monte Oliveto and Chiusure. On the way, the road has several car pull-offs, affording beautiful views of the **Abbey of Monte Oliveto Maggiore.** Enjoy a picnic, take in the sights and sounds, and catch a quick nap amid echoing church bells across the valley.

When visiting the Abbey itself, be sure to allow a couple of hours to explore. It is free to visit, and visitors are welcome to wander the grounds all day; but the church buildings are open only from 9 am to noon and 3 pm to 6 pm. The Abbey, founded by Bernardo Tolomei in 1313, is uncharacteristically built of mostly red brick. The grounds cover several acres, home to many Benedictine monks who established their own sub-order of Olivetans. The name is in honor of the Mount of Olives connected to the Christ story; the abbey

RISTORANTE MARIO

coperto E.150
.aqua E.150-200
vino casa E.600

guancia vitello   E.10.00
Anatra Pael. oTart.   E.18.00
fonsona   E.10.00
Osso Buco   E.10.00
coniglio   E.10.00
Pollo   E.6.00
Bistecca   E.12.00
Fiorentina Kg   E.35.00
B. Maiale   E.7.00
Trippa   E.9.00
agnello   E.10.00
Cinghiale   E.10.00

Pici, tagliatelle.
ravioli, tortellini,
spaghetti, penne,
ribollita, zuppa faro,
zuppa ceci, E.7.00

Cacciucco E.15.00
zuppa Polpo E.10.00
spaghetti scampi E.9.00

Rombo x 2 pers. E.35.00
Baccala E.10.00
Spigola E.12.00
Tonno piastra E.12.00

patate, insalata mista,
fagioli, verdura E.4.00

Bruschetta E.3.00
aff. Toscano E.6.00
aff. Toscano + formaggi E.10.00
Formaggi Misti E.8.00

Deser
Panna cotta, tiramisu
zuppa inglese, Catalana
crostata E.4.00
cantucci-vin Santo
E.5.00

appended "Maggiore" to its name once several other Olivetan abbeys were established elsewhere in Italy.

The church and surrounding buildings (including a museum) house some fine examples of Renaissance art, including a series of frescoes from 1505 by Antonio Bazzi, better known as "Il Sodoma." The frescoes line the entire four walls of the cloister and depict various scenes from the life of St. Benedict: "How Benedict Freed a Monk from Demonic Possession," "How Benedict Receives Maurus and Placidus," "How Benedict Banishes the Harlots from the Monastery," and so on. The images of Maurus and Placidus are actually young versions of Leonardo da Vinci and Alessandro Botticelli. Later abbots evidently decided that some images were not suitable, as several faces of demons and cats were scratched off of the wall, although the bit with the harlots stayed as is.

Il Sodoma (Giovanni Antonio Bazzi)

Though the nickname was originally given to him derisively by a rival painter, Bazzi himself proudly adopted "Il Sodoma" as his brand halfway through his career. He was prolific, having painted at the Vatican and other important sites in Rome and Siena. He also worked at the Abbey of Monte Oliveto Maggiore, painting a series of frescoes depicting the life of St. Benedict. As with any artist of the Renaissance (or any time for that matter), Sodoma painted what he was paid for, producing images both religious and historical, and often including animals and mythical creatures.

Continue wandering through the complex and head upstairs to the Monumental Library, housing centuries-old books on huge shelves, and the museum, which displays artwork from medieval times. Of course the church itself is huge and filled from floor to ceiling with paintings, frescoes, stained glass work, and intricately beautiful wood-carvings. The entrance to the Cantina is located on the back-side of the main church building. Open seasonally, it offers wine tastings and tours of the old winery, which includes huge casks and ancient wine-making machinery. The abbey grounds also include a store where many monk-made products are sold, including *liquori*, honey, tinctures, wine, and of course olive oil.

Continue on the way to and through Chiusure, and follow signs on the meandering roads to return to Trequanda. From Monte Oliveto it is only about 10 km to Trequanda as the crow flies. Thankfully, we are not crows, so we drive the little roads around the ridge of the Crete Senesi. This is the way to travel here: Wind and wander, explore, and discover. And don't forget the oil.

Trequanda

Il Conte Matto (The Crazy Count)
This fantastic restaurant offers their own wine and oil — you can sample both while gazing out over the vineyards and olive groves from their terrace. Conte Matto also offers rooms, so you can plan to have an 'epic' meal and then stroll right upstairs to sleep it off in one of their gorgeous four-poster beds.

Closed Tuesday, and late November.

http://www.contematto.it

Buonconvento

Da Mario
A small family run restaurant on the main street of Buonconvento. No menus, just a few dishes on offer each day. Ask what's fresh, especially for dessert — we got lucky with a hot tart straight out of the oven. Reservations advisable as seating is limited — stop in in the morning to ask for a table, then wander the town until lunchtime.

Closed Saturdays.

+39 0577 806157

La Porta di Sotto
Modern Tuscan cuisine, very friendly service, excellent wine list.

Closed Wednesdays.

http://www.laportadisotto.it/

Montisi

Ristorante da Roberto

Excellent restaurant in the medieval village of Montisi, which also offers a few rooms. Fresh, local, seasonal food.

Open mid March to mid November. Day off variable. Booking required. Open at noon, last seating just before sunset.

http://www.tavernamontisi.com/

Trequanda

Il Conte Matto

Absolutely stellar restaurant with beautiful rooms above, plant yourself here for a few days, explore the countryside during the day and work your way through the menu at night. Four poster beds in the rooms are a charming touch.

Restaurant closed Tuesdays, and late November. Double rooms from 60€. Breakfast in the restaurant for an additional 8€ daily.

http://www.contematto.it

Lucignano

B&B Cappuccini

This cute B&B is actually three separate apartments, located just outside the town wall in Lucignano. Each apartment has a small kitchen so you can cook for yourself if you choose, and all of the apartments have access to the beautiful garden with hammock and picnic tables. Lots of free parking and the wedding-cake shaped tiered town of Lucignano is just a 5 minute walk away.

Apartments from 70€.

http://www.icappuccini.it

B&B La Gianduia

Located right within the town walls, B&B Gianduia is blessed with tall ceilings adorned with elaborate murals. Breakfast is served in a common room that is also decorated with murals; it feels like dining in a museum. The owner explained to us that she keeps rates low because she wants travel to be affordable for people, what a refreshing and generous concept.

Rooms from 60€.

http://www.bedandbreakfastilgianduia.com/

Abbey of Monte Oliveto Maggiore

Abbey founded in 1313, with an incredible library, extensive grounds and famous frescoes by Sodoma. Plan to spend few hours here, there is plenty to see, including the monk's shop and a cantina where you can sample oil, wine and grappa made by the monks.

Open 9-12 and 3-6. Free entry. Check the Abbey's schedule if you are interested in seeing the monks sing in Gregorian chant.

Murlo

Etruscan Museum

Murlo is famous for its Etruscan museum, which is extensive, and appropriately so, as the people of Murlo have recently been discovered to share a significant gene pool with the ancient Etruscans. What better place to visit an Etruscan museum?

Open Tuesday - Sunday 10-1:30 and 3-7. Closed Mondays.

http://www.museisenesi.org

Buonconvento

Susy

Cute little shop on the main street of Buonconvento that sells knit goods, e.g. sweaters, scarves, mittens, hats, etc. Many of them are knit right there in the shop, look for the label marked "Susy".

Some unusual items here including some tube-shaped scarves, which are knit loose and thin like spider webs but are actually quite warm in winter.

Closed Sunday and Monday. Open in summer 9:30am-7:30pm; in winter open 10:30am-7:30pm. Open Sundays during festivals.

Abbey of Monte Oliveto Maggiore

Monk's Shop

On the grounds of Monte Oliveto Maggiore, this shop sells honeys of interesting varieties (ginger, lavender, orange, acacia, rosemary, thyme, pepper and more), plus soaps, liqueurs, tinctures, lozenges, homeopathic medicines, all made by the monks. There are also recipe books and travel guides for the area.

Open 10-12 and 3-6.

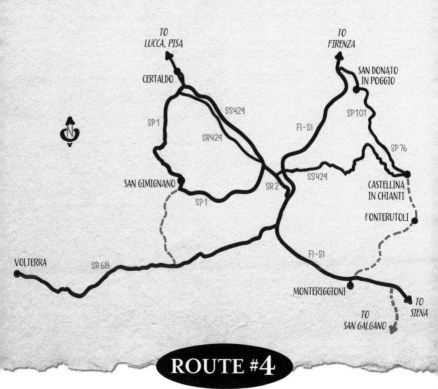

ROUTE #4

Central Tuscany
Western Chianti and the Val d'Elsa

The Firenze-Siena highway (the "FI-SI") runs directly north-south between the two cities. To the east are the dense forests and vineyards of the storied Chianti region; to the west is the lush valley and rolling hills of the Elsa river.

We begin outside a tiny medieval hill town on the western edge of Chianti, **San Donato in Poggio**. San what? Where? Never heard of it? Exactly. This picturesque and sleepy hill town (*poggio* means "knoll") has a few small restaurants and bars, and a shop or two. Its church at the bottom of the hill is small but beautiful.

It's a nice enough place to spend a few hours in its own right, but what makes it special is actually just outside of town, south on the SP101: **Locanda di Pietracupa**. This is one of our very top favorite restaurants as well as a place to stay. The rooms are modest but immaculate. The food is as fine as any Michelin-star restaurant anywhere. Brothers-in-law Luca and Massimiliano present their wives' beautifully made cuisine with impeccable service. Traditional dishes feature modern twists, in a postcard-perfect *terrazza* setting overlooking the San Donato "skyline" and its surrounding vineyards.

We've had more meals here than we can count. Often restaurants that focus on presentation do so at the expense of taste or quality, but not so here — everything is as delicious as it is beautiful. Particularly memorable dishes: a basket of *parmigiano* cheese filled with fava beans and chopped *salumi*; a *lasagnette* pasta noodle wrapped around an artichoke cream filling; a *sformato di caprino*, a

goat's cheese soufflé served with honey and ginger; *cipolle tropea*, a red onion baked with balsamic vinegar until it achieves a carmelized, chewy crust; and an unbelievably paper-thin and delicate *pappardelle* pasta. They also offer the memorable *bistecca Fiorentina*, a famously traditional plate throughout Tuscany. This is a VERY large cut of prized Chianina beef — the standard cut is three fingers thick—and should only be ordered by ravenous, rare-beef lovers. Desserts here are inventive and artful, so be sure to save room.

Staying upstairs in the Locanda's rooms for a few nights encourages sampling the whole menu over several meals and exploring the extensive, Chianti-centric wine list without the concern of driving after dinner.

Bistecca alla Fiorentina

The popular Florentine steak, "*bistecca alla Fiorentina*", is traditionally made from Chianina cows — the white longhorns grazing the hillsides of central Tuscany. This huge cut of meat — a porterhouse or T-bone — is carefully selected and dry-aged for days before being grilled for the diner. These are usually three fingers thick; they are served very rare, but with a dark char on the outside. They are priced either by the kilogram (1000 grams) or "per etto" (100 grams), so make sure you do your math before ordering. Also, you'd better be hungry.

And speaking of not driving: Luca stocks a few interesting *digestivi* (after-dinner liqueurs). Some of our favorites come from a maker, Emilio Borsi, located a few hours west near the Tuscan coast. One is made from oranges; another with vanilla, lemon, and milk (yes, milk — there's natural sediment floating in it); and another made from the bark of a tree, "*calisaja*," grown only in Ecuador. (See this *liquorificio* in Itinerary #6.)

During the day, range out to the south and west, into the Val d'Elsa, to visit several fascinating towns and their attractions. Winding south, pass through **Castellina in Chianti**, a beautiful, ancient town whose profile from afar is inexplicably

marred by a huge industrial feed factory. Close up, though, it's as lovely as any Chianti village. This is one of the three original cities that banded together to define themselves regionally as Chianti-makers in the 18th century. Wander through the charming old *centro*, and visit the Etruscan tomb on the outside of town. For a quick snack, stop by **Gelateria in Castellina**, an artisanal gelato shop on the SP76 just outside the *centro*.

Passing through Castellina, go just beyond the FI-SI highway to reach the walled castle town of **Monteriggioni**, Built in 1219, it has protected Siena from both Florence and Volterra over the centuries, and overlooks the ancient and well-

travelled Via Cassia road. The village is largely preserved, making it an almost perfect representation of a medieval fortified hill town.

The circular wall is less than 600 meters in circumference, punctuated by over a dozen guard towers. Visitors without vertigo can buy a ticket to walk the platforms atop the walls. A combined ticket gains admission to the medieval museum as well, where visitors can see and even try on replicas of armor and weapons from the ages.

The extreme care taken to preserve the town's historicity seems to give Monteriggioni a Disney-like quality, which, along with the easy accessibility, attracts huge crowds from April thru October. From November to March, though, it's nearly crowd-free, making it the perfect time to enjoy the museum and wall walk, the bars, and the many shops. Don't miss the hand-loom workshop simply named **Artes**, selling knit goods made on the premises.

The town has a full-on medieval festival in mid-July, with costumed musicians and artisans

doing things like they did in the 1300s. This may be the best or the worst time to visit, depending on personal tastes. In any case, it's a good idea to get there as early as possible to beat the crowds. (A larger version of this experience can be found in Volterra in August — more on this later on.)

Several lodging options are within the walls. Our favorite is the imaginatively named **Monteriggioni Castello**, a newly-done apartment decorated with antiques to give an old-world feel. The host Matteo is friendly and accommodating — he'll tell you everything there is to know about the area.

On the way in or out of the town, stop at **Bar dell'Orso** down the street, near the highway. Nondescript from the outside, the bar's interior charms visitors with floor-to-ceiling whimsical wood figures and sculptures carved by a local artist. The deli area serves up some of the best panini in Italy, with delicious local meats and cheeses on fresh-baked, crusty bread. The place is filled with locals at 8:30 am, many ordering an espresso and a grappa. (Yes, grappa.)

Far to the south of Monteriggioni lies a legendary location: The **Abbey of San Galgano**. The story behind this ruined abbey, and the still-intact church that looks over it, is interesting: Galgano Guidotti was a historical figure from the 12th century. The repentant Galgano supposedly plunged his sword, previously used only for nefarious

Coffee and the Bar Culture

Though coffee is not grown indigenously, the coffee house/bar culture has become an essential element in Italy's society. In addition to wine and various cocktails and liqueurs, every bar serves *espresso* — the little shot of very strong coffee — and the various drinks deriving from it: *Cappuccio* (better known by the diminutive *cappuccino*), named after the brown robes of Capuchin friars; and *caffè corretto*, an espresso with a shot of grappa added to "correct" for the caffeine boost. Some historians go so far as to suggest that the rise of the coffee house in Italy was a direct cause of the Enlightenment in Europe.

deeds, into the stone atop Montesiepi; the hilt created a cross, a sign of his newfound piety. As a result of this sensation, the man and the place became sanctified, visited by pilgrims and monks. This became the site of a round church which still stands today (and in which can still be seen the stone with the sword hilt protruding from it); word of the sword artifact undoubtedly spread quickly throughout the devout of Europe; it is possible that this was in fact the source of King Arthur's own sword legend. A few decades later, in 1218, a large complex was built in the valley below, becoming the Abbey of San Galgano.

The church is free to enter and visit; its round shape and domed ceiling make the space inside a great resonating chamber. Right next to the chapel is the "herbalist's shop", in which can be found many products (soaps, oils, jams, liqueurs) made by various local artisans or by other monastic colonies elsewhere in Tuscany.

The abbey ruins are open for a fee of €3 per person – well worth it, for a stroll through these haunting ruins. The abbey was mostly abandoned by the 1600s, and its roof and bell tower collapsed in the late 1700s, making it a source of stone for other local buildings until historians and archaeologists began the work of preserving the remains.

Returning to the FI-SI, head north and then turn west to **Certaldo**. It's worth noting here that many larger Italian towns, especially hill towns, have two sections: The *citta alta* ("upper city"), usually meaning the old, historic town *centro* at the top of the hill; and the *citta bassa* ("lower city"), usually a more modern buildup of businesses and residences. Here, Certaldo *basso* is a large sprawl; but look for the parking area that is marked with a pedestrian symbol and a sign for the *centro*, and be prepared to walk up the steep hill (10-20 minutes) to the old town. Alternatively, follow signs to park near the *funiculare*, ("cable car"), which takes two minutes and costs €2. Either way, the reward for the effort is yet another picturesque step back into Italian history. The well-preserved medieval and renaissance buildings are part of the town's ongoing effort to build and restore these old styles. The stunning views of the valley below make it obvious why this town, like so many Tuscan hill towns, was much fought-over for centuries.

Connected to the **Church of Saints Tommaso e Prospero** is the impressive **Museo Civico del Palazzo Pretorio**, a 900-year-old palace with an

extensive Renaissance art collection. Purchase a combination ticket for this along with the **Museum of Sacred Art** and the **House of Giovanni Boccaccio,** the Renaissance writer and 14th-century Certaldo resident.

When it's time for a break, consider the **Caffetteria Artistica (di Bar Boccaccio)**. This cute little place is a normal bar in every way, with one exception: the house specialty, "*Cappuccino Decorato*". When we ask for *due cappuccini*, the barista asks, "*Normale, o decorato*?" Though we've never heard of a "decorated coffee", of course we have to try it. The barista lovingly turns each cup into a unique work of art, using various gel icing and small candies to decorate the milk foam. All that decoration does nothing for the taste of the coffee, but watching the effort and seeing the result is an artistic adventure.

Continuing south from Certaldo, we come to **San Gimignano** (we refer to it affectionately as simply "San G"). This is a beautiful old city, distinctive for its multiple towers resulting from medieval nobility constantly trying to one-up each other in height and grandiosity. A bustling tourist destination, it's larger than most places we visit. Many guidebooks and brochures detail the usual attractions there, including climbing a couple of the tallest towers for a spectacular 360-degree view of the surrounding countryside.

The center of San G is dominated by two towers reminiscent of the World Trade Center. The larger of these is the Torre Salvucci, which is now available as a holiday rental. Staying here is extravagant, but it's not fancy. On the contrary, the logistics of moving up and down in this tower necessitates careful planning — "OK, which of us has the wine, and the glasses, and the corkscrew?" — and strong calves to propel up the nearly 200 steps to the rooftop 11 stories up. But there's a grand payoff: Sitting on the little rooftop patio with a glass of wine, some bread and cheese, looking down over the town, watching the sun set as the clouds roll by, the birds circling below us, you'll indeed feel like royalty from the middle ages.

Medieval Europe conjures thoughts of torture, and Europe has seized on a trend of opening torture museums, often in small towns. For those interested in the ugly underbelly of the Middle Ages — and who isn't? — the **Museo della Tortura** in San

G is worth visiting, especially in bad weather. The displays are detailed and graphic and may cause some to lose their appetite (or lunch) depending on the time of day. We suggest stopping for a glass of wine before visiting.

Speaking of wine, the lovely **Osteria del Carcere** is next to the torture museum. This small Osteria focuses on wine, paired with traditional dishes. The cheese plates, seasonal soups, and homemade pastas all score excellent marks. This is a good place to splurge on a nicer-than-usual bottle of wine and pair it with dishes recommended by owners Elena and Roberto. The family loves opera, which they always play in the restaurant. We love to watch them as they work, quietly singing with the arias under their breath.

On the other end of the main street is the old **Panificio Boboli**, a famous family-run bakery. In a town catering so much to tourists, Boboli remains staunchly traditional. For a meal away from the tourist crowds, seek out **Ristorante Mandragola**, a few blocks from the bustle. Their garden is a little haven of quiet amidst the bustle of the *centro*.

Driving farther to the west, the medieval fortress-town of **Volterra** beckons. This is another "small" hill town that we regard as quite large. The site of the city has been occupied since Etruscan times, as its Etruscan archaeological museum attests. Volterra was and is an important center for alabaster; many artisans in town work with the soft, white mineral. There is also a museum of medieval torture here, if you missed your share of bloodthirsty justice in San G.

An imposing fortress of the Medici family dominates Volterra. Built in the mid-1300s, the fortress enabled the ruling Florentines to maintain control of the city and its resources. Don't miss the excavated Roman theatre, built into a cliff on the edge of the old town. Over the centuries it had been gradually filled with garbage; it was then covered, grown over, and eventually forgotten. (As performers, we think sadly about what commentary this might have been on the culture of the time.) Not until 1951 was it rediscovered and excavated.

Plenty of accommodations dot the town. To escape the crowds, try **Il Portone,** a small garden-apartment complex a few minutes north of town.

It's just inside the Porta Diana, a 2nd century Etruscan gate. Walking up to the *centro* from here takes 10-15 minutes. It's fun to buy a few things in town and have a picnic in the garden, especially in Volterra's busier season. Enjoy an excellent meal at the out-of-the-way **Il Sacco Fiorentino**. Locals rate it as one of the best restaurants in town, so reservations are advised.

Again and again, we describe visiting some of these places in Italy as a step back into history. This is often the only way to describe the feeling of wandering through so many ancient and historic places. But Volterra affords a more literal option: Each August, the city holds its **Volterra 1398** medieval festival. Many Italian towns hold these kinds of events (like Monteriggioni, mentioned above), usually in the summer, but this is one of the most extensive, and highly organized in the country. All the townspeople dress in period costumes, and stalls throughout the town feature merchants, food vendors, and craftsmen doing things the way they were done in the Middle Ages.

These merchants only accept *grossi*, a coin minted by the town for the festival, designed to look like 14th century currency. These can be purchased at "banks" scattered through the town. In the town square,

groups perform hourly demonstrations of flag-throwing accompanied by bands of trumpeters and drummers. Each *contrade* ("neighborhood") has its own flag, and even its own specific tune and drumming pattern. The festivities  also include a falconry show, with demonstrations by several of your favorite raptors.

This entire itinerary includes several larger, more heavily-visited towns (though nothing like a Firenze, Siena, or Pisa). But thoughtful planning makes it more enjoyable to experience these grand historic places without getting pressed by the crowds. And if things get a little too busy, hop in the car and hit the countryside. Dozens of small towns in the beautiful Val d'Elsa await discovery.

A note about Firenze (Florence)

This chapter, and the next, bring travelers close to Firenze, probably the most popular — and most crowded — destination in Tuscany. Though it's far too large for our "Little Roads" travel style, our itinerary clients frequently decide that they want to spend a few days there. So, rather than covering ground that so many other books have already done, we'll mention just a few locations here — places that still feel like local spots.

To avoid the stress and cost of parking in the center, we like to use the new parking facility at Villa Costanza, to the west of town right off the A1 highway. From here a tram train takes travelers and commuters into the *centro storico* and all the tourist hotspots.

To the east of the town center, look for the street market of Sant' Ambrogio. To the side of the temporary market stalls is a tiny shop, **Semel**, where you can get a fresh, creative sandwich and a glass of wine for around 5 euro.

Cross the river on the Ponte Carraia. (Hint: The view of the famous Ponte Vecchio is actually much better from one of the other bridges.) Just down a side street you'll find **Francesco di Firenze**, a family-run leather shop with unique handmade shoes and other goods. Just a bit farther south you'll find **S forno Panificio**, a bakery offering the finest breads, pies, cookies, sandwiches and more — as well as serving light breakfasts or lunches. Everything here is of the most outstanding quality.

For lodgings, you can't beat the central location of Hotel Palazzo Gamba. Directly on the Piazza del Duomo, this hotel has a few choice rooms, and even a full apartment, with balconies facing Florence's famous cathedral and baptistery. The prices are comparable to other Firenze hotels, and the views of the Duomo from your own private balcony can't be beat.

WHERE TO EAT

San Donato in Poggio

Locanda di Pietracupa

One of our favorite restaurants in the world. Absolutely stellar food and impeccable service, set in the Chianti countryside. Beautiful dining room, large expansive terrace and a beautiful enclosed veranda as well. Best to arrive here as hungry as possible so you can try as many courses as you can manage. Extensive and well thought out wine and liqueur list. Do yourself a favor and book a room here for a few nights so you can explore Chianti during the day and this menu at night.

Open every day from Easter-October 31. Closed Tuesdays from November 1 - Easter, fully closed December 27-March 1. Rooms from 90€.

http://www.locandapietracupa.it/

Monteriggioni

Bar dell'Orso

Nondescript looking from the outside, this bar is well worth a visit to see the vast collection of funny wood carvings by a local artisan. Stop in for a coffee, or a light lunch in the dining room. There is a large deli case here and they'll make you an excellent panini or two to take with you as you explore the area. Open every day.

http://www.bardellorso.it/

San Gimignano

Osteria del Carcere

Charming Osteria just next to the Torture Museum, Via del Castello 13. Booking is a must as tables are limited. Soups here are excellent and the owners are big oenephiles so they have an extensive wine list and can recommend something excellent. The owners also love opera, which they have playing in the background all day; they hum along as they make your dishes.

Cash only - no credit cards.

Closed Wednesday, and no lunch on Thursdays. Closed January-March.

Locanda La Mandragola

San Gimignano has a lot of restaurants that cater to the tourist crowds, but Mandragola is one of the places locals go to eat. Food is locally sourced and traditionally prepared. There is a garden for outdoor dining in the warmer months. The restaurant also offers a few rooms upstairs.

Open every day for lunch and dinner.
https://www.locandalamandragola.it

Panificio Boboli

We include this bakery because we found the most exquisite salted caramel cookies here, and focaccias that were both crunchy and soft, just perfect. The bakery has been open since 1909; you'll want to stop here to pick up a picnic lunch or grab some sweets for breakfast. This is a good place to stop for treats, but also to learn about local history through food.

Open Mon-Sat 6am-8pm and Sunday 6am-2pm.
https://www.facebook.com/panificioboboli/

Fonterutoli

Osteria Fonterutoli

The Mazzei family has been making wine since 1435 and now has several vineyards, in Chianti, the Maremma, and Sicily. It's possible to try several of their wines with each dish over lunch, a sort of self-styled wine tasting, using the menu as a guide. After lunch, head across the street to their cantina to sample and purchase their wine and grappa. If they have tiramisu on the menu, ask if it's served in a little flower pot with cocoa cookie "dirt"; it's the cutest dessert presentation ever.

https://www.mazzei.it

Volterra

Il Sacco Fiorentino

Many locals told us this was the best restaurant in Volterra. Located on a small side street in the old town, Via Turazza 13, Sacco Fiorentino has a large dining room but in warmer months sets up a makeshift patio across the street, flush with the church's side wall. Booking advisable in high season.

Closed Tuesdays.

Castellina in Chianti

Gelateria Artigianale L'Antica Delizia

Gelateria on the outskirts of town making their own gelato and sorbet using the best available materials. We love the raspberry/rosemary gelato.

Open 11am-8pm; Closed Tuesdays.

http://www.anticadelizia.it/

San Donato in Poggio

Locanda di Pietracupa

One of our favorite places to stay, this Locanda has four well appointed rooms that are located directly above one of our all-time favorite restaurants. Nestled in the Chianti hills outside San Donato in Poggio, it's hard to find a more restful, peaceful place.

Double rooms from 90€.

http://www.locandapietracupa.it/english/index.-html

Volterra

Il Portone

Set just outside Volterra, Il Portone provides a series of self-catering apartments to rent. A large communal garden space covered by an ancient wisteria makes the perfect spot for an afternoon snack or do-it-yourself al fresco dinner. It's a 10-15 minute walk uphill to Volterra, but it's a calm, peaceful place with plenty of parking. It's especially pleasant during summer season or crowded festival weekends when tourists fill the town.

Apartments from 660€ weekly but shorter stays are possible.

http://www.residenceilportone.com

San Gimignano

Torre Salvucci

San Gimignano is known as "Medieval Manhattan" for its iconic medieval towers, and in this case, you can stay in one! The entire 11-story tower is yours, including an unforgettable rooftop patio. It's not the most comfortable or convenient lodging (rooms are fairly small since it is, after all, a medieval tower), but it is a once-in-a-lifetime kind of place.

From 215€/night, three night minimum stay.
http://www.torresalvucci.it/home-eng/

Monteriggioni

Monteriggioni Castello

This is one of those places we've found that feels to good to be true. It's an entire house, with gorgeous wood-beamed ceilings, decorated with antiques. It's just steps from the church, on the main street in town, but tucked away in a corner so it feels like a private oasis. Owner Matteo lives next door and is incredibly welcoming, you'll feel at home right away.

The home is on several booking apps.
From 90€/night.

WHERE TO SHOP

Monteriggioni

Artes

Wool weaver shop within the town wall. The front room is a showroom for the knits (scarves, jackets, sweater, hats, capes) and the back room contains the loom where all the fabric is made. Many of the scarves bear the distinctive stripe pattern of this shop. The material is extremely soft and warm.

Monteriggioni

Armament museum and town wall

This museum is located within the town wall, a fantastic visit for children and still a lot of fun for adults. Multiple rooms house armaments like chain mail, swords, helmets and the like; visitors are allowed to try them on. The town wall is incredible, a brief walk, but those afraid of heights should be aware in advance that the walkway is made of see-through metal grate, so don't look down!

Wall walk only: 2€. Museum only: 3€. Combo ticket for both: 4€. Museum and walk; Closed Tuesdays.

Certaldo Alto

Museo Civico del Palazzo Pretorio

Housed in a 900 year old building in the picturesque town of Certaldo Alto, this museum highlights works of Pier Francesco Fiorentino, and also has a medieval torture chamber and prison.

Open April-September 9:30-2 and 2:30-7:00; October to March, 9:30-4:30. Tickets: 6€.

San Gimignano

Museo della Tortura

Extensive torture museum just off the main square. It's relatively small and expensive as far as these types of museums go, but it is informative as a good reminder of what not to do. Expect lots of tourists at any time of year as San Gimignano is a touristy town and torture museums in general are clearly geared for the tourist set.

Open July-September 9am-midnight; mid-September to July 9am-7pm.

Entry 10€.

San Galgano

Abbey of San Galgano and the Sword in the Stone

While this Abbey, the first gothic church built in Italy, now sits in ruins, it is still incredibly beautiful. On the hill overlooking it you'll see the chapel housing the Sword in the Stone, possibly the origin of the King Arthur legend. If you're alone in the chapel, take a moment to hum to yourself — the sound bounces off the round walls in the most unusual and disconcerting manner. Next door to the chapel is a monk's shop where you can buy liqueurs, oils, candies, and medicines made by monks. They have a eucalyptus liqueur here we have been unable to find anywhere else.

The chapel and shop are free to enter, the Abbey costs €3 and is open every day from 9am-6pm.

Volterra

Volterra 1398 Festival

An extensive medieval festival that takes over the entire town of Volterra in the end of August each year. This is by far the most involved festival we've seen, with trumpeters and drums, flag throwers, medieval games, crafts and food, its own currency, and the townspeople all in costume. If you want to visit this we recommend staying overnight, and staying somewhere outside the town wall (like Il Portone listed above), so you can avoid the traffic, have a clean bathroom to use, and have a place to rest during the heat of the day. We had a fantastic time at this festival doing just that, but if we had just driven in for the day I think the experience would have been overwhelming.

Held the 3rd and 4th Sundays in August, Tickets are 10€.

http://www.volterra1398.it

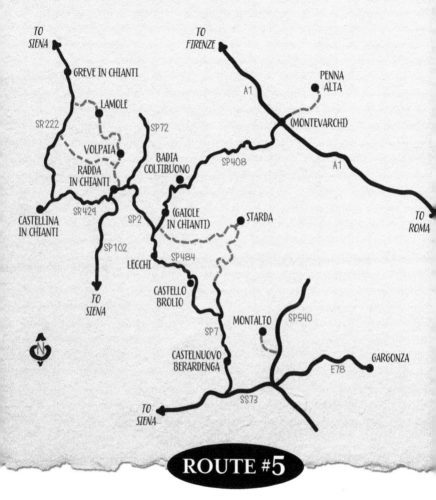

ROUTE #5

Central Tuscany
The Chianti Region

Chianti is a region, a wine, and a way of life in these rolling forested hills between Firenze and Siena.

The people here take their wine very seriously. It's a pride that dates back to the 14th century, when the term *Chianti* referred to wine made in the mountains south of Florence. In the early 1700s, three cities — Castellina, Radda, and Gaiole — became known officially as Chianti-makers, and the status of the region solidified. The region has since expanded, but strict rules and oversight still govern the making of Chianti. This includes everything from the types of grapes (primarily *Sangiovese*) to the method of growing, fermenting, and bottling, to the appellations of specific varieties based on the hillside where the grapes originate. Even the bottling and labeling has tight regulation. Historically, Chianti came in a *fiasco*, the iconic squat bottle with the wicker basket base. Chianti Classico, identifiable by the *gallo nero* ("black rooster") logo on the bottle label — is the "premium" version. It's more expensive but noticeably better, even to those of us who are *non-sommeliers* (French for "not sommeliers").

All this is to say: Chianti is a good place to drink wine.

We begin at the beautiful **Castello Gargonza** in the southeastern section of Chianti. Gargonza is a preserved 13th-century medieval castle nestled deep in the woods. Its lodging and restaurant are popular for weddings and other events, and it is easy to see why. Particularly memorable is the *risotto di prosecco e fragole*, an unexpected (and untraditional) risotto dish with *prosecco* (sparkling white wine) and strawberries.

The rooms range from single hotel-like spaces to efficiency apartments to fancy bridal suites.

Every room has windows that open to the beautifully cool night or early morning air and the sounds of the surrounding forest. The grounds of the castle are meticulously kept and, in season, bursting with flowers.

Chianti Classico

One of the most famous Italian wines is the Tuscan Chianti. Many foodstuffs in Italy are labeled with acronyms, like IGP (*Indicazione Geografica Protetta*) or the more exacting DOP (*Denominazione d'Origine Protetta*), for foods made with specific traditional methods and sourced from certain regions; and DOC (*Denominazione di Origine Controllata*) for wine. Various nationwide consortiums maintain the standards for these designations. The black-rooster-labeled Chianti Classico is made under such rigorous standards as to earn the DOCG label — *Denominazione di Origine Controllata e Garantita*, which we choose to translate as "satisfaction guaranteed".

Drive west through the woods on the beautiful Senese Aretina highway (known alternatively as E78 and SS73, in the typically confusing Italian manner). At the village of Colonna di Grillo, turn north toward the **Castello di Montalto**. Since the 11th century, this large walled castle and grounds served as important strategic elements in the perpetual conflict between Siena and Florence. A large battle in 1208 resulted in countless deaths, while the castle suffered damage in this and many other conflicts over 300 years. Today, owners Diana and Giovanni peacefully live here year-round. They run an *agriturismo* (olive oil and honey are among the many products made here), renting out many of the rooms and towers to guests.

The Tower Room over the castle gate is a charming apartment in the former guard tower. In fall and winter, it's not unusual to hear hunters

in the surrounding wooded hills, trying to bag the *cinghiale* that's served at dinner later. Castle guests can be sparse this time of year though it lures large group events at other times of the year. A couple of walks through the woods, and a couple of nights in this ancient place, add up to a truly magical experience.

Montalto is near the significant town of **Castelnuovo Berardenga**. Founded in the 1300s as a Sienese defensive outpost, this town has a few interesting sights. Not much of the original castle remains, but check out the last remnants of the clock tower, which is open to the strong-winded for climbing. Modern murals decorate some of the walls on the street; each year new murals are drawn corresponding to the plays that the town theatre company is producing that season. Also check out the ornamental Renaissance garden and beautiful landscaping outside the **Villa Chigi Saracini**.

Castelnuovo Berardenga is also home to a couple of worthwhile food stops, just to the north of the historic *centro*. **Bar Quei 2 da Carlo e Claudio** specializes in grilled meat dishes and also serves fabulous desserts. This place is popular with the locals, so a good bet is to make your reservation in the morning for lunch, then return to claim your table after poking around town.

Continue north on the SP484 and look for the turnoff to the **Castello di Brolio**. On the way up to this 800-year-old castle is its restaurant, **Osteria del Castello**. Its lovely patio is filled with the sounds of the forest, including a brook that runs down the hill past a small-scale model of the castle. The Osteria proudly makes the point that all of their food is organic, seasonal, and sourced lo-

cally. In fact, the restaurant's olive oil and wines come from that very hillside, as Barone Ricasoli (the Brolio brand) is one of the region's most well-regarded producers of both. After lunch, you can wander up to the castle for a visit and sample the castle's wines in their *enoteca*.

Look for a turnoff to the northeast, into the heart of the Chianti region, towards **Starda**, a tiny medieval village at the end of a winding dirt road. The village was a medieval fortification belonging to the Conti Guidi family, and much of the old architecture is still on display. Today only nine people reside in the town, which is basically owned by the family operating **Osteria Starda**. A destination hardly gets more remote than this, and even in Chianti, the food rarely gets better. Everything is handmade, and the menus are hand-written daily depending on what's fresh. The dining room is dark and romantic, with stone walls that seem to exude mystery and tradition. The food is freshly prepared, and in the slow season, often by the same person who seated you and took your order. Given the remoteness of the area

and the extremely high quality, it's surprisingly affordable. Plan for a long lunch. Everything is made to order, and the pacing allows time to savor the atmosphere and the food. For dessert, Luisa recommended the just-made *biscotti* dipped in *vin santo*, a sweet dessert wine, also made on the premises. The establishment also sells its own wine (Chianti Classico of course!), olive oil, *grappa*, and *vin santo*, all sourced from the acreage in their own little valley. Best to arrange a reservation ahead of time, so they'll know you're coming. It's not uncommon to be the sole diners on any given day, so if they're not expecting you, they might not be around. For those who enjoy a remote, peaceful location, lodging is available in the village.

Relatively less remote but still off-the-beaten-track is **Badia Coltibuono**. This walled abbey and church in the woods was established in the 11th century. The name is derived from the words *buono raccolto* meaning "good harvest"; indeed, the grounds are the source of many fine wines and other local foodstuffs. Today the abbey operates as a hotel, and its ancient buildings and formal gardens are open for tours. Its excellent on-site *ristorante* offers locally-produced Chianti cuisine in a romantic setting.

A jaunt east on the SP408, all the way past the Al *Autostrada*, takes us to the vicinity of Penna, and

Biscotti and Vin Santo

The Italian word *biscotto* simply means "cookie" and can be any kind of crunchy baked treat. Most people usually use the word in reference to *cantucci* — the hard, oblong cookies that are very common in any Italian baker's window. Historically this durable cookie was made for the benefit of travelers — "durable" is derived from *duro* meaning "hard". In recent times it has become a frequent dessert offering, once someone got the idea to soften them by dipping them in tasty beverages like coffee or Vin Santo — the latter, "holy wine", is a common dessert liqueur made by most winemakers.

the hilltop village of **Penna Alta**. Perched on the side of the hill is **Il Canto del Maggio**. This family-owned restaurant/*agriturismo* is part of the "Slow Food Presidium", a loose network of restaurants who are devoted to presenting high-quality food from local, organic producers — many of their offerings they produce themselves. Plan to settle in for a long, epic meal here — all the food is hand-made with care. Several of the pages in the menu are explanations of the chef's philosophy, details about the slow food movement, and specifics on every farm and vineyard they purchase their products from. This place is a diversion from the rest of this route, but it's worth it.

Return west on the winding roads until you come to **Radda in Chianti**. This is the center of the Chianti region, one of our favorite places to visit in the area.

The town itself is a well-preserved, medieval walled city with plenty of restaurants and shops. It's fun to find the medieval walkway that runs underneath some of the buildings. Radda's main church, **Propositura di San Niccolo**, sits above the town's central piazza, across from the **Palazzo del Podesta** (formerly the town hall, now a hotel). Originally built in the 13th century, the church houses a wide range of sacred art that spans centuries. Look for the glass case to see part of the original medieval castle wall upon which the church was built.

Rooms are available above **La Bottega di Giovannino**, a little *enoteca* and shop near the west edge of town. The room overlooks the town wall and a beautiful wooded valley to the west, so sunsets are an event in themselves. Benches line the walkway along the wall, a fine place to sit and take in the expansive views.

Next door is another unique lodging, the **Art Rebus Tower**. A renovated 13th-century tower, it's decorated with quirky modern art, and enjoys a patio several stories above the street — a good place to escape and get above it all, while still being in the thick of things.

Radda offers many dining options. The excellent **Le Forchette** is just outside the town wall. Popular with locals, this tiny, popular family place serves fantastic homemade food, like artichoke and *pecorino* lasagna (its thin, pastry-like noodles bear no resemblance to what Americans call lasagna). Save room for the "Italian cheesecake" if they have it — unlike the New York version, this one tantalizingly falls apart like a warm brie.

A bit more upscale is **La Botte di Bacco**, a restaurant on the south wall with a dining room overlooking another stunning valley view. An extensive wine list and impeccable service pair perfectly with modern Tuscan fare. Try *involtini* of eggplant, grilled eggplant slices and prosciutto wrapped around *mozzarella burrata* and a balsamic reduction. It's so good we've replicated it at home many times.

For a lighter bite, or just a quick coffee or *amaro*, make a stop at **Pasticceria Gelateria Sampoli & Lapis** on the east edge of town, across from the tiny town park. The bar serves a delicious variety of baked goods, many made in-house. We are always envious of those who work here; of the tantalizing all-day aroma of *biscotti* and coffee, and of the stunning view out of the window behind the bar.

For food shopping, it's tough to beat **Porciatti**

Alimentari. This extensive, family-run *alimentari* is on the main Piazza, sporting a big green neon sign across from the town park. The store stocks perfect picnic items: local cheeses, salumi, and house-made salads and spreads, plus fresh local bread, cakes and pastries. Produce, olive oil, water, and wine are also available. This store ranks as a favorite because of the high-quality selection of locally made items, including biscuits, cookies, cheeses, and chocolates. The owner's son recently opened up **Enoteca Casa Porciatti**, just a few steps away, down the medieval walkway — another great place to stop for local wine and samples from the family delicatessen.

Just a few minutes east of Radda is **Chianti Cashmere Goat Farm**. Set in the heart of the Chianti hills, this farm is home to a herd of adorable goats, as well as a shop stocked with fine cashmere cloth and quality goods made from their wool. The hosts here also offer lunches and teaching visits for kids and adults alike. Go for the experience, and come away with a gorgeous and unique memento from your trip to Chianti.

To the northwest of town, the SP2bis road winds through the woods. Look for Lucarelli, a town of just a few buildings... Oops! Too late, you drove through it. Turn around and get lunch at **Osteria Le Panzanelle**, another favorite of the locals. A chalkboard outlines each day's special

Pici — Tuscany's own pasta

Originally made with just flour and water and with no extruding device, this hand-rolled pasta is the epitome of Tuscany's "*cucina povera*" (that is, peasant cooking; literally, "poor kitchen"). These long, thick noodles, nowadays usually made with the extravagance of a bit of egg and some salt but still rolled by hand, are ubiquitous throughout central Tuscany; the pasta style originates from perhaps as far back as Etruscan times. Today *pici* can be found on many Tuscan menus, offered several ways, including *all'aglione* (a tomato/garlic sauce) or *alle briciole* (oil-soaked, baked breadcrumbs). If it's *fatto in casa* — made in-house — you can't go wrong.

dishes, and lunch in their vine-covered garden is a timeless experience.

To the south of Radda, off the SP408, is another special eatery, **Ristorante Malborghetto**. The food here is all *biologico* (organic) and carefully sourced from local producers, including from the restaurant's own garden. Driving north from Radda, consider a stop at **Volpaia**. We came to see this town's castle and to look for the Etruscan ruins that we heard were nearby. We never made it past **Bar Ucci**, where owner Paola Barucci (the name of the bar is a play on her family name) entertained us with great conversation and strong homemade *grappa*. Paola also serves light lunches of *panini* and pastas that are highly recommended by the locals. Volpaia is a very tiny town, basically a few houses and this bar at the bend of a road. We'll have to return to see the sights another time, but we suggest a stop for coffee, a homemade sweet, and perhaps a big glass of grappa lovingly and generously poured by Paola.

The highway continues north, gradually climbing one of the many grapevine-covered hills until it finally reaches the remote hilltop town of Lamole, **Ristoro di Lamole**, run by business partners Fillipo and Paolo, affords tremendous views from the patio (on a clear day San Gimignano is visible in the distance). The food is beautifully prepared and presented. As with many of the best places, the menu is small, with everything carefully designed. While waiting for a table, Filippo may bring an "*amuse-bouche*" from something they're playing with in the kitchen, or maybe a little plate of pecorino with local jam. Pastas are, of course, handmade. What might be a pedestrian dish in another restaurant is here a culiinary experience — for instance, they make their own sausage and salami. Desserts are equally well-conceived. This is a good place to simply trust your server — the *cameriere* — and ask what he recommends for that day. The extensive wine list is thoughtfully chosen. On occasion, the restaurant hosts small wine tastings, and one of their Chianti Classico varieties is made right there in Lamole. With dessert, try a *grappa* made from that same wine. Make reservations in advance via email, and ask for a patio or window table for the best views.

Desserts here are excellent as well — they have a great molten chocolate cake that must be ordered ahead of time. Their wine list is extensive and  carefully chosen — the restaurant hosts small wine tastings from time to time, and one of their Chianti Classico varieties is made right there in Lamole. With dessert, you can have a grappa made from that same wine. Reservations can be made in advance via email — you can ask for a patio or window table for the best views.

Driving down the other side of the mountain — another winding, narrow road — we come to the largest town in this wonderful wine region, **Greve in Chianti**. The town has a wine museum and dozens of wine shops offering tours and tastings of the famous Chianti vintages.

What is different in Greve is the lack of a town square. It's actually triangular, and a couple of interesting shopkeepers sell their wares under its porticoed walkways.

There's the **Antica Macelleria Falorni**: Prominent in the central piazza of Greve, this butcher shop has occupied this same building since 1729, and has been run by the same family since 1806.

They source only local animals from farmers that they know personally, and they use traditional methods in preparation of their meats (including the use of Chianti wine!). Tastings are available in the shop, which is a great spot to put together picnic fixings, including their own *salumi* and *prosciutto* of Falorni. They are well set-up for tourists with a few shelves of pre-sliced salumi, vacuum-packed and ready to go — perfect for picnic lunches or to bring home to cook for   dinner. Just outside the store, little paper brochures in four languages explain the history and operation of the *macelleria*. On the same block, the lively **Osteria Mangiando Mangiando** serves up local and traditional Chianti cuisine right on the main square. This Osteria focuses as much on sourcing their food as they do on preparing it — they consider high quality ingredients to be the cornerstone of their cuisine. Every vendor and farmer is listed on the menu; it's like a lesson in local quality.

Just a few kilometers to the west of Greve is the untouched town of **Montefioralle**. A walk through this tiny village is a must for lovers of picturesque Italian streets. Among the beautiful doors here, look for the ancestral home of Amerigo Vespucci — you'll know it by the wasp ("*vespa*") insignia over the door. To the north of Greve, another goat farm, **Podere le Fornaci**, is worth another diversion — but these goats produce milk for cheese. The

shop on the premises sells all sorts of varieties, every one of them delicious. "Eating locally" doesn't get more local than this.

The Chianti region was a war-ravaged territory for centuries with the residents of Florence and Siena both fighting over it. The legend of how the final lines were drawn between the two city-states is the origin of the black rooster icon, the Chianti Classico mark of excellence. At some point in the 1200s, both governments resolved that, on an agreed-upon day, a rider would set out from each city, one from Florence riding south, the other from Siena riding north. Where they met would become the undisputed territorial marker. It was agreed that the riders would begin at the first crow of the first rooster at dawn. Everyone agreed that this was fair. But some Florentines decided that "fair" was perhaps overrated: They got together and lit thousands of candles right outside the hen-house in question, creating such a light that Florence's big black rooster awoke in the dead of night. He began crowing, giving the Florentine rider a head-start of several hours, therefore enabling him to claim a much greater territory than the Sienese rider,

who started when their white rooster crowed at the actual crack of dawn. As a result of this advantage, Florence established what became the most powerful kingdom in Italy for centuries — although that didn't stop the warfare.

Happily, this tradition of conflict and bloodshed has since been replaced by traditions of artistry, great food, and fine wine, and of preserving traditions and the land of Chianti itself.

WHERE TO EAT

Gargonza

Ristorante Castello Gargonza

Truly incredible restaurant on the beautiful ground of the Castle of Gargonza. Remote, peaceful location. The large dining room has been converted from a barn; the view over the valley is incredible. A romantic setting; we recommend staying overnight at the Castle for full effect.

Closed Tuesdays, and occasionally more often in winter. Reservations recommended.

http://www.gargonza.it

Castelnuovo Berardenga

Ristorante Bar Quei 2 da Carlo e Claudio

Right on the main road as you drive into Castelnuovo Berardenga. Great little restaurant with nice desserts; if you've eaten elsewhere you can always stop here for a nightcap and a slice of cake or torte. Restaurant is quite busy with locals so reservations are a good idea.

Closed Wednesdays.
http://www.ristorantequei2.com/

Starda

Osteria Starda

Fantastic restaurant located in tiny Starda, with just 9 residents. Hand written menu that changes daily; restaurant offers their own oil, wine and grappa from their groves and vineyards. Stunning location, incredible food, traditional style. Reservations highly recommended, as the location is so remote.

http://www.castellodistarda.it/site.html

Radda in Chianti

Le Forchette

Sweet little restaurant located by the town wall, near all the public parking. Great views over the valley, nice cozy dining room. Limited menu, as everything is made by hand and to order. Good idea to book in advance as seating is quite limited.

Closed Thursdays.

La Botte di Bacco

Upscale restaurant located on the main street of Radda. Traditional Tuscan cuisine with a modern twist. Very attentive service and romantic dining room.

Closed Wednesday, and January 7-February 28.
http://www.ristorantelabottedibacco.it

Volpaia

Bar Ucci

Sweet little bar/restaurant in the tiny hamlet of Volpaia, which is just a small collection of buildings. Gregarious owner Paola Barucci is hilarious and welcoming. Homemade cookies and pastries can be found here, plus an incredibly strong house made grappa that is not for the faint of heart. The bar has just a few tables set aside in a separate dining room and offers a few dishes for lunch. Highly recommended.

http://www.bar-ucci.it

Lamole

Ristoro di Lamole

Absolutely not to be missed, stellar restaurant in the tiny village of Lamole. Gorgeous views, incredibly good locally sourced food, one of our favorite restaurants in Tuscany.

Open every day from March 1-October 31. In November, lunch only, and closed Wednesdays. Closed December-March.

http://ristorodilamole.it

Badia a Coltibuono

Ristorante Badia a Coltibuono

Located on the site of the monastery (now hotel), this excellent restaurant serves traditional Tuscan cuisine with a modern flair. Very romantic setting. If you are one of the later dinner guests, once the crowds have evaporated, a wild boar might emerge from the forest begging for scraps.

Mid March - late April, closed Mondays; Apr-Nov open daily; Nov-Jan open Thurs-Sunday only.

Castle Brolio

Osteria del Castello

Excellent restaurant just down the hill from the imposing Castle of Brolio. reservations highly recommended as opening times vary and this upscale restaurant is quite popular.

Closed Thursdays and January- mid March. Open for lunch and dinner in summer and fall; late fall and winter reduced hours.

http://www.baronericasoli.com/restaurant

Penna Alta

Il Canto del Maggio

Very off the beaten track, extremely high quality slow food restaurant in a tiny hamlet. Well worth any diversion from your established route.

Closed Mondays.

http://www.cantodelmaggio.com/

Greve in Chianti

Mangiando Mangiando

This restaurant is right on the famous triangle-shaped town square, and focuses on using organic, local ingredients. To say they focus on using local ingredients is really understating it: research and procurement is a central tenet of their philosophy. The menu lists where they find all their goodies so you know they take it very seriously.

They have a sister restaurant in Firenze if you

miss them in Greve. Reservations recommended.
http://www.mangiandomangiando.it/

Lucarelli

Osteria Panzanelle

Beautiful little restaurant in a town with about 8 buildings; a local friend directed us here and told us this is where the Chiantigiani eat. Traditional food, lovingly prepared, ask for a table in the garden when the weather is nice.

Closed Mondays.
http://www.lepanzanelle.it/

Lecchi

Ristorante Malborghetto

Tucked away in the tiny village of Lecchi, this upscale restaurant offers artfully prepared dishes (often using veg from their own garden) on a beautiful and flowerful patio. They specialize in truffles so if that's your jam, you'll want to book a table here. It is also possible to take a cooking class here with chef Simone Muricci.

Closed Tuesdays.
https://www.malborghetto.net/

Gargonza

Castello Gargonza

Remote, beautiful 13th century walled castle set in the woods. Double rooms up to full suites. Free wifi in the common area where breakfast is served, lovely garden area here as well. In summer there is an in-ground pool for guests. Small shop offering soaps, oil, and other local products. Stellar restaurant on site.

Rooms from 100€.
http://www.gargonza.it

Montalto

Castello di Montalto

Beautiful remote castle set among olive groves on one side and woods on the other near Castelnuovo Berardenga. Owned by the same family for generations, who live on site. Double rooms and suites for multiple guests available, some with working fireplaces and kitchenettes. No restaurants nearby so it's necessary to drive to dinner or cook your own.

Rooms from 98€.
http://www.montalto.it/index.shtml

Radda in Chianti

La Bottega di Giovannino

Small family-run place just above the family's restaurant of the same name. Very clean rooms tastefully appointed with great views over the valley surrounding Radda. Located within the old town;

easy free parking just a block away. Free wifi.

Double rooms from 60€.

http://www.labottegadigiovannino.it

Badia a Coltibuono

Badia a Coltibuono hotel

Absolutely gorgeous rooms in a renovated monastery in the Chianti hills. Excellent restaurant on site. In summer months, there is a formal manicured garden and a large in-ground pool for guests.

Open late March-November.

Doubles from 135€

Radda in Chianti

Art Rebus tower

Right in the center of town, this 13thC medieval tower has been restored and renovated and is now a very nice full apartment. It's remarkably affordable too, considering all you get, including a balcony that overlooks the main street. You can find it on several booking apps.

From $123/night.

Radda in Chianti

Porciatti Alimentari

A favorite stop of ours, Porciatti Alimentari (just across from one of our favorite bars) has an extensive collection of locally sourced beans, chocolate, wines, liqueurs, pastas, cheeses, meats and more. A great place to stop to pick up a picnic lunch, and to find goodies to bring home.

Open every day 8:00-1:30 and 4:00-7:30; Sunday open 9:00-12:30

Greve in Chianti

Antica Macelleria Falorni

Traditional butcher, right on the town square, open in the same location since 1729. No one does it better than these guys, who have been passing down the tradition literally for centuries. Easily accessible for tourists, as there are pre-packaged options of salumi and cheeses ready to go for picnics or plane. For the chef the options are endless. Incredible just for the smells.

Open 8:00-7:30; Closed Sunday.
http://www.falorni.it

Podere le Fornaci

This goat farm just outside Greve makes several kinds of goat cheese; it doesn't get fresher than this if you're looking for picnic or dinner items. It's possible to book a lunch here if you prefer not to cook. The little shop also sells local honey and jam. Opening days vary so check ahead before you visit.

http://www.poderelefornaci.it/

Radda in Chianti

Chianti Cashmere Goat Farm

We love goats, so here's another goat farm. This one raises goats for their wool, which they turn into the most deliciously soft cashmere. This is the largest cashmere goat farm in Europe. It's possible to book a lunch here as well, and you will likely have a chance to feed a baby goat. Open Monday-Friday from 4-7pm, but best to check ahead on their social media for updates.

http://www.chianticashmere.com/en/

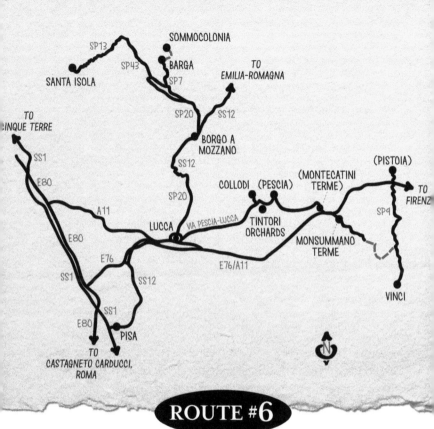

ROUTE #6

Northwest Tuscany
Pisa, Lucca, and the Garfagnana

Aside from Pisa with its gravitationally-challenged tower, the northwest region of Tuscany is relatively neglected in many Italian itineraries.

Nevertheless, it has a tremendous amount to offer, from a sandy beach coastline to the mountainous beauty of the **Garfagnana** region and from a citrus grove with bowling-ball-size oranges to the homes of Leonardo da Vinci and Pinocchio. Natural beauty and Italian charm are everywhere.

On the way from Rome to the Garfagnana, we find a few key places to stop. We begin on a quest to visit the source of one of our favorite artisans, **Emilio Borsi Liquori**. We sampled several of the products of this *liquorificio* when we ate — and drank — at the "Destination Restaurant" Locanda Pietracupa (see Itinerary #4).

A note on *liquori*: Italians tend to favor a type of after-dinner *digestivi* called *amari* (literally, "bitters") that are typically distilled from various herbs, fruits, or other plants. They're often dark brown, and vary from quite sweet to very *amaro* indeed. We like them all, but the varieties at Borsi really expand one's palate.

The shop is in a quaint little hilltop town, **Castagneto Carducci**. As the town is quite near the coast, savvy diners here will want to include *frutti di mare* (literally, "fruit of the sea" or seafood) among their menu choices. The coastal towns and beaches in this area are popular summer holiday destinations for Italians and foreigners alike, but in the off-season many of these places are quite empty. Castagneto Carducci is easy to park in, quick to get in and out of. It's a lovely place to walk around and explore.

Amari and other after-dinner drinks

It is common to finish a large meal with a *digestivo* — a shot to help everything settle in the stomach. This can be a *grappa*, a *vino dolce* (sweet dessert wine), or our favorite, *amaro*. The word *amaro* simply means "bitter", but it also refers to herbal *liquori* as well as a whole range of distillations: dandelion, rhubarb, pinecones, wildflowers, bitter oranges, artichokes, you name it — if it grows locally, someone will make an *amaro* out of it. Though some of them (like Averna or Montenegro) have a bit of sweetness, others tend to be quite bitter; you can actually order an *amaro amaro*.

Back to Borsi's liquorificio: Visitors who display significant interest and enthusiasm about *liquori* may be invited to tour the shop and then the back rooms where they concoct diverse elixirs. Their wares include two different kinds of *amarancia* (orange liqueur), and a lovely and unique liqueur called "*Liquore di Pastore*," made of lemon and milk and tasting just like a *panna cotta* dessert. This liqueur has milk sediment at the bottom of the bottle, which makes a shaken bottle look like a snow globe. Perhaps even more interesting is their bitter, herbal "Elixir China Calisaja." The base of this *amaro* is an Ecuadorian bark shipped to the store in big bags that look like mulch. In addition to their *liquori*, the store sells foodstuffs like pastas, oils, honeys and jams, as well as chocolate truffles, biscuits, and *panforte* (a Sienese-style, heavy cake) made with their liqueurs. They also stock multiple types of house-made grappa. Over the years we have brought back quite a few bottles from Borsi, much to the delight of our dinner guests.

Just to the south of Castagneto Carducci (and north of Suvereto), at the top of a long, winding road, is the charming **B&B Belvedere**. It is part of the tiny hamlet of Belvedere, just a few buildings surrounding a very small town square. Belvedere (which literally means "good to see") is so named because it offers an incredible view of the surrounding countryside from its perch atop the mountain. The B&B is very comfortable and quite affordable. The first floor houses a small restaurant perfect for a long, relaxing dinner. Sample local meats and cheeses of the Maremma (this southwest coastal region), and handmade pastas. In summer it's possible to dine on the patio or enjoy a bottle of *prosecco* while watching the sunset before dinner. (We did this in the dead of winter, while the staff watched, mystified.) The restaurant serves breakfast in the morning—leave time to admire the variety of artworks adorning the restaurant's walls. They are made by a local artisan and available for sale.

From here make quick work of the kilometers on the drive north, bypassing most of the coast-lands in order to reach **Pisa** early enough to beat the tourist traffic. There's a little parking lot down a small side street (Via Andrea Pisano) just to the west of the *centro*; from there, walk just a few blocks east to the famous **Piazza dei Miracoli**. This is where the square's Romanesque Baptistery, the medieval Cathedral, and of course the **Tower of Pisa** make it clear why tens of thousands of people flock to this location daily. It really is stunning and impressive. We suggest trying to get the earliest tour-time of the day, before the tour buses storm the town in full force. It's best to get tickets early, online — only by luck might you get a walk-in spot in one of the tower tour times. Groups of 20 climb the steps to the top of the tower, where the views — and the tilt — are truly breathtaking. It's easy to spend many hours exploring just the incredible architecture and inspired artwork in these three buildings themselves, let alone the rest of this historic and beautiful city.

Nevertheless, iconic beauty or no iconic beauty, we suggest getting out of there before the crowds make you crazy.

Back in the car, continue north to **Lucca**. About two thousand years ago, the Romans built this city on the site of an even earlier Etruscan settlement. At one point standing as the capital of Tuscany, it developed into a thriving medieval market town, especially prominent in the silk trade. Of course, to stay prosperous in medieval Europe, a city had to defend itself, and the large walls built for that purpose still remain intact. Today they are the most beautiful and ancient tree-lined greenway anywhere, perfect for strolling on foot or traversing on a bike. At a leisurely pace, cycling the entire circuit around the town would take about 45 minutes, not including picture-taking stops. Park just outside the North entrance, Porta Santa Maria, where just inside the gate a couple of bike shops offer hourly rentals.

At the center of town is the **Piazza dell' Anfiteatro.**Its unusual circular shape outlines its origin as a 1st-century Roman amphitheater and the site of many gladiator competitions. In medieval times the surrounding buildings were the center of the city's defenses, including gunpowder caches, salt stores, and a prison.

Just behind the amphitheater is **Osteria Baralla,**

which prides itself on serving typical Lucchese cuisine. One Lucchese specialty is *castagnaccio*, a dense cake topped with pine nuts. This is a centuries-old recipe, made from ingredients that were typical before Europeans developed their collective sweet tooth. Wheat flour and sugar were not readily available in this region, so it is made with chestnut flour and sweetened only with honey. Served with a scoop of unsweetened ricotta cheese, the *castagnaccio* may come off as an almost savory dish, but it doesn't get any more authentic than this. It's typical to see a few elderly Lucchese gentlemen sitting by themselves eating their after-lunch cake; so consider following the locals' lead.

If you missed the **Erbario Toscano** shop in San Quirico d'Orcia (from Itinerary #1), there is another one here: A perfumery and soap maker. There are generally a dozen or so scents available for purchase in soaps, perfumes, reed diffusers, candles, hand wipes, and other items. The scents are powerful and long-lasting, and they make memorable souvenirs or gifts. Beware that the black pepper candle will earn attention of TSA agents upon re-entry to the United States. A waxy, black rectangular candle with a very long wick looks rather like a block of C4 with a fuse.

A few more of our favorite spots in Lucca include four of its many churches: The **Basilica di San Frediano** was established in honor of an Irish saint who came to preach in Lucca in the 6th century. Its remarkable facade is a huge golden mosaic depicting Christ and the Apostles. (Don't miss the biblical scenes carved on the giant marble 12th-century baptismal font, inside.) The **Chiesa di San Michele in Foro** isn't just a huge church with a stunning facade; it oversees a wide-open and busy piazza in the center of town, where townspeople (and their dogs) gather to socialize and share news. (Puccini fans might want to grab a coffee or cocktail at the bar across from the church, Café Turandot.)

Parts of Lucca's Duomo, the **Cattedrale di San Martino**, date as far back as the 11th century; much of it was completed in the 14th century. The adjacent bell tower was already in place, so the cathedral facade needed to be "scrunched" to fit into the space. The church is incredibly ornate, inside and out - frescoes, carvings, and sculptures adorn

Leonardo da Vinci

He didn't need a real surname — the bastard born to a middling lawyer and a peasant woman became known simply as Leonardo of the town of Vinci. He was an artist, inventor, and philosopher of such astounding genius and accomplishment that the term "Renaissance Man" was seemingly invented specifically for him. Contemplating his genius becomes even more difficult when we learn that he never had a formal education other than basic reading, writing, and math.

almost every square inch of the building. On the east edge of town, the often-overlooked 14th-century **Chiesa di San Francesco** is an important stop on the Via Francigena pilgrimage route that crosses the country. Attached to it are the cloisters of a monastery that house medieval tombs and (of course) a statue of Saint Francis.

After so much church-going, you might be hungry. The **Antica Bottega di Prospero** food shop has been run by the same family for several generations. Here's where to find the best in local products - pastas and grains and nuts, jams and sauces, flour, dried beans and lentils and mushrooms, and of course lots of local wine, oil and *liquori* to choose from. If you're staying for a few days and want to stock your kitchen, or if you just want a few things to bring back with you to enjoy at home later, this shop is a perfect place to stop. Or, check out the beautiful goodies at the upscale bakery **Pasticceria Pinelli**. Grab a few *frittelline di riso* - sugar-coated rice fritters, a local specialty -

and go sit a few blocks away next to the bronze statue of the master cellist Luigi Boccherini, outside the Istituto Musicali di Boccherini, where you can listen to the students practicing.

Lucca has countless options for staying overnight. We recommend splurging a bit for the **Appartamento La Torre**, in the center of town across from the famous Torre delle Ore (clock tower). The several flights up to the apartment are worth the climb; at the top is a covered patio with sweeping views of the entire city. As it has a small kitchen, lodgers can cut the cost a bit by eating in and taking full advantage of such a stunning location.

Before driving north into the Garfagnana mountain region, divert east for a few interesting stops. The town of **Vinci** is the birthplace of the famous painter, sculptor, architect, mathematician, engineer, musician, biologist, cartographer, all-around genius and general show-off Leonardo. Much in the town is devoted to cashing in on his awesomeness. It's fun to explore the **Museo Leonardiano**. Craftsmen and engineers have painstakingly built or recreated many of the machines and devices that Leonardo invented and sketched in his many drawings and designs.

The museum sits near the top of the hill and offers the best view of the town and surrounding countryside. Outside the museum is interesting as well. The piazza is designed with modern, thought-provoking sculpture and architecture, meant to pay homage to the great master. It is extremely unusual to find new, modern art in these historic old sites, so this is a refreshing spot.

On the way back, don't miss the artisanal chocolate shop **Slitti Chocolates and Coffee** in the otherwise unremarkable town of **Monsummano Terme**. This internationally award-winning shop, halfway between Lucca and Florence, began as a coffee roaster in 1969 and expanded to include artisanal chocolates in 1988. Today it's a local treasure, and makes a wonderful stop, including the best cappuccino to enjoy with very delicious handmade chocolate. They offer a nearly infinite collection of chocolate: bars, truffles, creams, and chocolate spoons for coffee, as well as elaborate chocolate art, like enormous Easter eggs or Christmas candies. The artisans pay attention to every detail, from the raw ingredients used to make the chocolate and coffee down to the glamorous packaging. Slitti is a fun, memorable stop; it's also a great place to buy something upscale (while still being delicious and local) as a gift.

Tucked away down a side street on the outskirts of the small town of **Pescia** are the **Tintori Citrus Orchards**. Run by the same family for generations, "Il Giardino degli Agrumi" is open for self-guided tours. The greenhouse is home to hundreds of ornamental citrus plants, some more than half a millennium old. There is a small gift shop to buy honeys infused with lemon or orange, marmalades of many varieties, and body products made with citrus oils. It's prohibited to pick citrus off the plants, but the smells are plentiful. It feels like an incongruous experience wandering through a citrus orchard in cool northern Tuscany.

Just a few kilometers away is **Collodi**, the home of author Carlo Lorenzini (Carlo Collodi). It's a very small town completely dedicated to the story of Pinocchio. Skip the cheesy *Parco di Pinocchio* (€12

entry), the town itself is free to visit and is worth a stop just for the numerous murals illustrating the life and times of the little lying wooden bastard.

Returning to the main route, head to the edge of the Garfagnana mountains, north through **Borgo a Mozzano**. This town is best known for its **Ponte della Maddelena** ("Mary Magdalene's Bridge), an 11th-century footbridge that was a marvel of medieval engineering. It spans the Serchio river in three lopsided arches, giving it a

strange and twisted look that earned it the nickname *Ponte Diavolo*, or Devil's Bridge.

Climb the narrowing gorge of the Serchio river, to reach the heart of the Garfagnana mountains and the most prominent town here, **Barga**. The topography made the town a historically important strategic position, commanding views of the valley. Consequently the main feature of Barga is a fortified, walled city overlooked by its Romanesque *Duomo*, a cathedral dedicated to St. Christopher.

Cars are not permitted in the *centro*; visitors must park outside and carry luggage into the heart of the old town. Although there are various lodgings — B&Bs, hotels — try an apartment called **Toscana Nobile**, which is owned by a couple of American college professors living in California. The place is huge, suitable for three or maybe even four couples. It has a fireplace, a grand piano, and a terrace (three very unusual treats) as well as a full

Farro

Increasingly popular among foodies in the U.S., farro has been common in Tuscan cuisine since even before Etruscan times; monks in abbeys like Monte Oliveto Maggiore, as well as secular farmers, cultivate this most ancient wheat grain. Cooked whole, it has a texture similar to pasta cooked *al dente*, but its flavor is distinctive and delicious. A few bags of farro can easily be brought home in your suitcase — in addition to broadening the culinary offerings of your kitchen, it makes great packing material to pad the bottles of wine and oil that you'll want to bring home as well.

kitchen. Staying here imparts a real taste of what it must be like to live in Barga, to truly live in Italy.

This makes it possible to cook at home in the apartment's full kitchen, well-stocked with provisions from several neighborhood stores. For dining out, **Trattoria l'Altana** is a simple, family-run place just a few blocks away, still in the old *centro*. They serve cuisine typical of the Garfagnana: Handmade pastas with *sugo di cinghiale* (wild boar sauce), delicious meat dishes, and of course good local wine and oil.

Many peaks and valleys form the Garfagnana. It is heavily forested and very steep, so fog tends to cling to the countryside, making for mysterious vistas. On a clear day, though, from Barga's *Duomo* it's possible to see across the mountainsides to neighboring villages.

The highest in view is tiny **Sommocolonia**. Drive the very small winding roads up to that village, to discover a memorial for victims of the September 11, 2001 attacks. It seems the residents love Americans because of the great heroism of the U.S. 92nd Infantry Division members, who died while keeping the strategically located town out of Nazi hands in December 1944. The soldiers holed up in

the town were part of an all-black detachment of the segregated 92nd Infantry Division (the "Buffalo Soldiers"), so the Army brass paid little attention and they were left there to surrender or be killed. But one of the key figures in this resistance, US Army Lt. John Fox, directed Allied artillery to his position in order to destroy the oncoming Nazi troops. He perished in this barrage along with his comrades, but halted the enemy advance. A marker in the field just below the town commemorates Fox. He was one of several of this division who was awarded a posthumous Congressional Medal of Honor for his heroism, bestowed not at the end of the war but in 1997.

One last spot, about 30 minutes to the west of Barga, is worth at least a quick look. A bend in the highway reveals a small lake, colored a weirdly Caribbean turquoise blue. On its banks is **Isola Santa,** a tiny, remote village with an interesting story. The town dates to the 13th century and was built on the banks of the river Turrite Secca, which flows into the Serchio. Being quite off the beaten track, this medieval settlement remained relatively unchanged as centuries passed it by. In 1949 a company built a hydroelectric dam near one end of the village, creating a lake and submerging much of the town. The remainder of the town (including its church) was soon abandoned, and only in recent years has extensive reclamation and rebuilding occurred. Walk one of the paths through and around the town. A few spots offer glimpses of the submerged buildings, a ghostly reminder of what the town once was.

Isola Santa is a good metaphor for the Garfagnana region — and for many of the places that we love to visit: Out of the way, often forgotten, but a beautiful place for those who take the time to explore the little roads of Tuscany.

Lucca

Osteria Baralla

In the heart of the medieval city lies this excellent Osteria serving very traditional Lucchese cuisine. Frequented by locals, lively, casual atmosphere.

Closed Sundays.

http://www.osteriabaralla.it

Osteria Miranda

Incredibly charming restaurant decorated in a quirky style, serving traditional Lucca dishes with a modern twist. Its location away from the most popular tourist spots adds to its "hidden" charm. Service is top notch too.

Dinner only, closed Mondays.

+39 0583 952731

Pasticceria Pinelli

Traditional bakery with the best cream puffs you will ever find in your life. You'll be spoiled for choice here; we love to search out places like this that remain unchanged by tourists and travelers and still do things the same way as when they started (in this case, in 1939). Perfect.

Closed Mondays.

http://www.pasticceriapinelli.it/

Ristorante Giglio

If you're looking for an upscale, elegant, and creative dining experience, Giglio is for you. Of course the ingredients are top quality, but what you're really paying for here is the imagination of the chef. We found ourselves mesmerized by our dishes and by those of the diners around us. A culinary experience for the adventurous. Hours vary by season so check their website.

https://www.ristorantegiglio.com

Barga

Trattoria L'Altana

Traditional food of the Garfagnana served in a relaxed, cozy environment. Located within the town walls. Limited tables so reservations are advised.

Closed Wednesdays.

WHERE TO STAY

Lucca

La Torre Apartment

Located right in the center of town, this apartment has everything you need: bedroom, kitchen, living room...but the real reason to rent it is its stunning, gorgeous balcony. From this covered tower balcony you get a 360° view of the town. We spent every night up here eating and drinking and watching the sun set; it is magical. Highly recommended·

The apartment is on several booking apps so search for it by name. Host Barbara is friendly and kind and keeps the place sparkling clean.

From 50€/night.

Suvereto

B&B Belvedere

Cute, comfortable rooms in the tiny town of Belvedere, which is just a collection of about 6 buildings at the top of a big hill. Great views, peaceful environment, excellent restaurant on site.

Double rooms from 60€.

http://www.belvederedisuvereto.it

Barga

Toscana Nobile

Huge, spacious private apartment in the heart of old Barga. Working fireplace, full kitchen, small balcony. Parking in town lot (for a fee) about 5 blocks away, you must bring your luggage from there.

Prices vary by season.

http://toscananobile.com

Pisa

The Field of Miracles

Arrive early in the morning to avoid busloads full of tourists, who will begin showing up mid-morning. Easy, cheap parking is available just 2 blocks away on

Via Andrea Pisano. Buy your ticket in advance online for the Tower — groups of 20 are let in every 15 minutes. Children under 8 are not admitted. Children 8-10 get in for free (ID may be required). Children 10 and over pay full price.

Tower tickets 18€.

http://boxoffice-info.opapisa.it/index.php?id=482&L=1

Vinci

Museo Leonardiano

Museum in the heart of old Vinci highlighting the town's most famous resident. Panoramic terrace offers the best views of the valley around. Terrace open March-October.

Open November-February every day from 9:30-6:00.

Open March-October every day from 9:30-7:00. Terrace open 11:00-6:30.

Tickets 7€; 5€ for children 14-18; 3.5€ for children aged 6-14.

http://www.museoleonardiano.it

Pescia

Tintori Citrus Orchards

Citrus orchards in the heart of Tuscany with hundreds of varieties of all types of citrus, some of which are over 500 years old. Small shop on premises where you can buy honey, soda, jams and personal bath products made from citrus oil. Self guided tours available of the orchards for 4.5€.

Open year round 8:00-12:30. Open in winter 2-5 and summer 3:30-7; fall and spring 2:30-5:30.

Closed Saturdays November-January and July-August. Closed Sundays June-February. Closed all holidays and festivals.

http://www.oscartintori.it

Castagneto Carducci

Emilio Borsi Liquori

A small liquorificio whose delicious goods can be found in restaurants all over Tuscany. Liqueurs are made in the back rooms; if you are very nice you may get an impromptu tour. Well worth a stop if you like unusual liqueurs and products made from them.

Closed Sundays, and Monday afternoons.
http://www.borsiliquori.it/sito/

Lucca

Antica Bottega di Prospero

Five generations of the Marcucci family have tended this shop, which sells local wine, oil, beans, farro, spices, mushrooms.....This is a perfect place to stop for a gift for yourself or someone special. A treasure trove for food lovers. The inside of the shop is like a museum as well, incredibly charming.

Open 9:30-7:30 every day, Closed Sundays.
http://anticabottegadiprosperolucca.myadj.it/v/anticabottegadiprosperolucca

Tommasi Loom Works

Weavers work on ancient looms in the back of the shop during the day, so you can stop in and watch this art being created. Several different lines of clothing are on offer at any given time; obviously those change with the season.

Open 10-1 and 3-7 every day, Closed Sunday.
https://tommasiloomworks.com/?lang=en

Monsummano Terme

Slitti Chocolates and Coffee

Award-winning artisanal chocolates and coffee. Stop off for a cappuccino and sate your sweet tooth while shopping for gifts for family and friends.

Open 7:00-1:00 and 3:00-8:00 every day except Sunday. Closed most of August.
http://www.slitti.it

Pescia

Tintori Citrus Orchards

Unusual citrus orchard tucked away near the town of Pescia. Take the self-guided tour of the ancient orchards, then stop in the small shop afterward.

Hours vary wildly each month, so be sure to check the website.

4.50€ to enter orchard, free to enter shop.
http://www.oscartintori.it

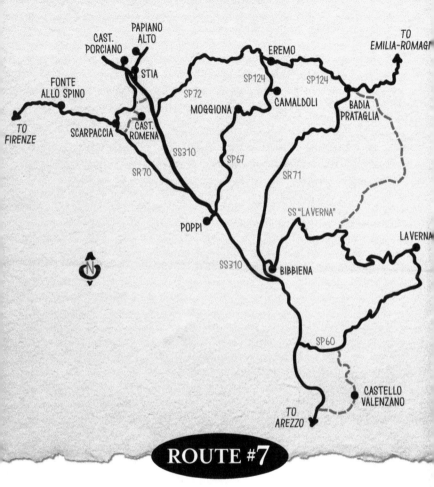

ROUTE #7

Northeast Tuscany
the Casentino

Almost as overlooked as the Garfagnana are the mountainous, forested northeast reaches of Tuscany's Casentino region.

At the top of this immense valley is the source of the Arno River, the same one that snakes south and then back north and west to bisect Firenze before continuing west all the way to Pisa and the Ligurian Sea. Some of the Casentino's Apennine peaks are more than a mile high. The smaller, more manageable hills became strongholds for the powerful families of the medieval era, most notably the Counts Guidi, longtime rivals of the Florentines.

Begin this drive at the southern part of the Casentino. Off of the SR 71 north of Arezzo, a winding tree-lined road leads to the stunning **Castello di Valenzano**. More than a thousand years ago, a fortification was established here to overlook the ancient road along the Arno River. It was built up over subsequent centuries, falling into the hands of various factions as wars determined local power. It has been in the Rondinelli family since the 18th century, when major renovations and design created the present building — a neo-Gothic storybook castle. Take a magical stroll through the grounds, admiring the mixed architecture, taking in the aroma of the fruit trees and wood smoke from the restaurant's grill, and enduring the glares from the gargoyles adorning the walls. Look for the recurring crest featuring a flock of swallows — the sigil of the Rondinelli family. Visitors can lodge in the castle for reasonable rates and enjoy a romantic restaurant on-site. It serves up beautiful plates of traditional regional cuisine, specializing in wood-grilled meat dishes.

Continuing north, we visit **Bibbiena**, one of the few medieval hill towns of any size in the area without a castle. Consequently, most tourists skip this town, giving visitors the chance to experience an authentic feel for life in this region. Its central Piazza Tarlati (named for a local power family of

yore) bustles with local color. History and archae-ology buffs will want to amble through the small but enlightening **Museo Archeologico del Casentino**, which displays eons of history, from prehistoric times to the Roman era. Several churches dot the town and showcase well-pre-served Renaissance and medieval artwork. The **Church of San Lorenzo** contains two tableaus by the famous Renaissance ceramic artist Andrea della Robbia. His work can be found all over the Casentino and throughout Tuscany.

Andrea della Robbia

Visitors to sacred sites all around the Casentino and throughout Tuscany will get used to seeing the distinctive blue and white ceramic artwork of Andrea della Robbia. He was the apprentice of his uncle Luca, and he became the undisputed master of this art form. His students, including his own son Giovanni, carried on his artistic methods, creating a "della Robbia" tradition that influenced generations of artists in this medium.

Down a little side street in the medieval centro, seek out the excellent **Ristorante Il Tirabusció**. This place is part of the "Slow Food Presidium", a loose network of restaurants devoted to presenting high-quality food from local, organic producers, who are highlighted in the menu. For specially marked dishes on Tirabusció's menu, like seasonal *testaroli e pesto*, (a thick, pancake pasta), a portion of sales supports the Slow Food movement. This cozy, casual, relaxed place caters to tastes of the locals with great ingredients from the surrounding countryside.

Just a 5-minute drive from the Bibbiena *centro* is the **Santuario di Santa Maria del Sasso**. This 14th-century church was built following a purported vision of the Virgin Mary on this site.

The church contains a ceramic piece by della Robbia, but the real interest here is the way the church was built around the living rock; one stone juts out of the floor behind the altar. The walls of the crypt below are raw stone as well; one area is a shrine where devout visitors leave notes of prayer for loved ones, in hope that the Madonna who once appeared there will grant their wishes.

For those interested in religious history, an excursion east into the hills is a must. Winding and climbing through the forest for a half hour or so leads to the remote, 12th-century **Santuario Franciscano de La Verna**. An extensive village in itself, it seems to have been piled precariously on the rock mountainside. The site marks an important religious pilgrimage destination and makes a fascinating tourist stop, so get there early or in the off-season.

The sanctuary has several churches, chapels, and shrines as well as lodging for the resident priests and nuns in charge of its care. At the top, a stark wooden cross dominates a cobbled *piazza*

overlooking the valley to the west; a walk down a few dozen steps leads to a cold stone cave. Saint Francis of Assisi resided here for some time and is said to have received the stigmata here while meditating in his grotto. His room and one of his tattered monk's robes have been preserved for visitors to see.

Scattered all over the sanctuary walls are more

ceramic pieces by the aforementioned della Robbia and his artistic heirs, as well as a long hallway with frescoes depicting different episodes of St Francis' life.

Returning to the Arno River and continuing north, the **Castello di Poppi** soon comes into view. This is the central town and castle of the Casentino. Built in the 12th century, it was the stronghold of several generations of Counts of the powerful Guidi family during medieval times. It was eventually taken over and expanded by the Florentine power structure. Inside this architectural marvel is a treasure trove of medieval and Renaissance art, ancient manuscripts in the library, the obligatory bleak prison rooms, and stunning views from the top of the bell tower. The inner courtyard walls are covered with the coats of arms of the various Florentine governors who took up residence here over the centuries. One room houses a museum piece displaying the Battle of Campaldino, a huge-scale military action fought in 1289 AD, which was a key battle between the rival political factions of the Guelphs & Ghibellines. The taxing climb to the top of the main tower offers 360-degree views of the countryside. Keep an eye on the time when you're up here: the tolling bells can be powerfully loud when they ring out the hour for the entire valley to hear.

In the 11th and 12th centuries, two of the dominant factions in the conflict between the Papacy and the Holy Roman Empire were the Guelphs (Team Pope) and the Ghibellines (Team Emperor). These conflicts began as a classic clash of Church and State, but the two groups continued their animosity for several more centuries, leaving their mark on Tuscany's history in the Casentino, as well as other places in Tuscany and Emilia-Romagna to the north. Many historic sites saw bloody power struggles between the two groups who attempted to control the strategic riverways and hilltops of the region.

For high quality and affordable lodging in Poppi, the excellent **Albergo San Lorenzo** sits at the foot of the castle, outside the old walls. The building is built on the hillside around an 11th-century chapel, which is used today for events and art exhibitions. Many of the hotel's rooms overlook the valley to the south and east. The best room has a lovely, expansive balcony, perfect for a snack and a bottle of wine in the evening. In good weather, a typical Italian breakfast is served on a beautiful covered terrace.

Just below the castle, Poppi's *centro* is small and tight, with a porticoed main street and many shops and restaurants. Tucked down a side street is **L'Antica Cantina**, an establishment built, as the name implies, in an ancient wine cellar. The low brick walls and ceilings make this a romantic place

to enjoy traditional and seasonal fare, with hand-made pastas and (of course!) an extensive and varied wine list.

Other sights include the **Oratory of the Madonna del Morbo**, a hexagonal building in the middle of the central *piazza*. The 10th-century **Chiesa di San Fedele** houses ancient artwork and, in the crypt, the remains of Torello, a favorite son of Poppi. On the road up the hill to the town is a

large World War II monument whose pillars are reminiscent of buildings in the Roman Forum.

Still farther upriver from Poppi is another hilltop castle, this one in ruined splendor: The **Castello di Romena**, another Guidi stronghold. Its ghostly remains still have an aura of the power and nobility. Its two towers,—one a prison, the other a keep—at either end of a large cypress-lined courtyard overlook the valley in all directions. Some say that Dante Alighieri was a guest here (in the keep, not the prison!), and he writes about it in his *Inferno*. A "Master Adamo" was a resident of Romena, where he was hired by the Counts Guidi to make fake Florentine coins. The dukes of Florence discovered the plot and executed Adamo, hence his presence in Dante's hellscape.

From the castle it's a short drive or a moderate stroll down the hill to the stunning **Pieve di San Pietro di Romena**. This church was built in the 12th century on the remains of an earlier (8th-century) religious site. Remnants of the older one can be seen in the church's crypt space under the sanctuary. Take particular note of the capitals of some of the columns, depicting people, animals, and otherworldly creatures. One capital commemorates the *Tempore Famis*, the Time of Famine of 1152. The date is inscribed in Roman numerals on the column. This historic calamity inspired the religious-minded (which, back then, was basically everybody) to even more piety. The church sits on the edge of a tiny village, the Fraternità di Romena, a religious pilgrimage retreat. The church's stunning location in the heart of the Casentino valley makes it easy to see why it is such a destination for the devout.

Meander to the SR70 and head west along the road to Consuma, back in the direction of Firenze. This is another winding rural road with stunning views of the Casentino forest hills at every turn. Make a stop at **Bar Scarpaccia**, named for the village that is just a cluster of buildings at a crossroads. This all-purpose bar-restaurant —*salumeria-tabaccheria*-post office is a popular meeting place for the locals. It is also regarded as one of the best sources of locally produced cured meats, especially *finocchietto* (fennel salami) and *prosciutto* made from wild boar (*cinghiale*) of the Casentino. Enjoy a drink and a *panino* for a real taste of the local food coupled with an authentic feel for the local life here.

For a more standard, sit-down restaurant setting, the **Locanda Fonte allo Spino** is just a bit further west on the same road to Consuma. After miles and miles of woods and valleys, you'll be sure you missed it, but don't turn around; it finally appears from seemingly nowhere. This is the kind of place that locals come for a special Sunday

lunch. Given the out-of-the-way location, it's clear people take eating here seriously. The Martini family, in the restaurant business for several generations, offer traditional local dishes in a light and cheery atmosphere. The adjacent shop sells all manner of locally produced foodstuffs.

Returning yet again to the Arno river valley, continue north to the mill town of **Stia**. Situated directly on the river, this town used water-power to become an economic powerhouse, producing the region's famous cloth in its wool mills. The extremely durable and strong Casentino cloth has been made here for some seven centuries. Initially the Franciscans used the cloth for their monastic robes and other mundane purposes, but today it is a hallmark of high fashion to wear a colorful coat or cloak of this material. A central source for these products now is **Tessilnova Wool Merchants** in the old mill building. It offers plenty of high-end materials such as mohair and cashmere in addition to goods made of Casentino cloth.

A short drive north from Stia leads to another tiny hilltop hamlet and the tower of **Castello di Porciano**. Originally another Guidi outpost protecting the river and Stia, this 11th-century tower is now a museum and residence. The first three floors are devoted to exhibits on local history and culture, spanning antiquity to recent times. Many residents of nearby farms and homesteads have brought old family artifacts for display here — ancient farming equipment, household tools, and weaponry — to show a slice of family life in the Casentino. Dante was famously a guest at this castle as well, as several displays attest.

The upper floors house the owner's residence. Martha Specht is the daughter of George Specht, an American officer, and Flaminia Goretti, an Italian nurse, who met in the aftermath of the Second World War. (George was from North Dakota; one display case contains items of Lakota origin, very incongruous in a medieval Italian castle.) George and Flaminia's love story is featured in the museum displays, and the tower stands as testament, casting its shadow across their gravesite in the family cemetery just outside the walls.

The Specht-Goretti family has recently converted many of the surrounding buildings — on the remnants of the old castle walls — into vacation rentals. They make for an out-of-the-way stay in this beautiful region. The tiny village lacks bars and restaurants, but a scant 10-minute drive takes the hungry traveler to another nearby village, **Papiano**. It's home to the big dining room and lovely patio of **Trattoria da Loris**, one of the region's most popular restaurants. It offers an assortment of handmade pastas with various sauces, but don't miss the house specialties: "*scottiglia*", a spicy stew of beef, rabbit, pork, and chicken, falling off the bone; and "*acqua cotta*", a traditional soup that varies depending on what's in the kitchen at any given moment. Both are typically served to large tables of boisterous locals, so eating here feels like a true Italian experience. It's casual and relaxed, and steeped in the traditions of generations of residents. The menus are only in Italian and the staff speaks little or no English. But don't worry, if you're not that comfortable speaking Italian: Everyone here is very friendly, and eating here is worth any amount of pointing and gesturing. Just

remember three words: *"Scottiglia, per favore!"*

Departing from the path of the Arno, climb east through more forested hills to reach another local food destination, in the tiny hamlet of **Moggiona**. Here the owners of **Ristorante Il Cedro** serve local and seasonal dishes, prepared according to their *Casentinesi* family traditions. Specialties are *funghi* (mushrooms, common in these forests, served on *crostini*) and handmade pastas with sauces made from the daily spoils of the local *cacciatori* (hunters). They also stock several *liquori* from the nearby monastery, so it's a good place to sample a couple (but not if you're the driver) before continuing to their source, just a little farther up the hill.

Scottiglia and Acqua cotta

These are two of the most popular "peasant dishes" of the Casentino: *Scottiglia* is a delicious savory stew of multiple meats, including beef, chicken, lamb, and sometimes wild boar, or even rabbit, or venison (depending on what the forest hunters have been up to lately). The meat is served in a dish with *bruschette*, which are *"fare la scarpetta"* — to sop up the spicy, flavorful sauce. *Acqua cotta* — literally meaning "cooked water" — is a hodgepodge of various ingredients in a brothy soup. Both dishes exemplify the *cucina povera* of Tuscany — simple, local, seasonal, delicious.

The **Monastero di Camaldoli** was founded in the 11th century, and the monks here are doing things much as they did a thousand years ago. They produce honey, *liquori*, and many other foods, while attending to their ancient devotions. Set deep in the dense and fragrant woods, this is a beautiful and quiet setting. It's a destination for many religious travelers seeking refuge and solace, as well as a fruitful stop for those looking for a bit of unspoiled history. The church here is stunning, ornately decorated with frescoes and various artworks from across the centuries, including work by the famous Renaissance artist Giorgio Vasari.

A must-see is the **Antica Farmacia**, the old pharmacy. A great stop for stocking up on many monastic products, the shop also has a museum component. On display are antique machinery, intricately carved wooden doors and walls, centuries-old anatomy texts with drawings of internal organs, and a stuffed alligator. (Yes, an alligator. Why?) We love the *liquori*. here; our favorite is

"Laurus 48," an aromatic herbal *digestivo* made from an ancient recipe — the ingredients on the label are listed in Latin!

Camaldoli's village has a small bar/restaurant, as well as modest lodging, making it not only a pilgrimage spot but also a waypoint for hikers and campers traversing the many footpaths of the expansive Apennine mountain range.

Just a mile or so north of the monastery, even more remote in the forest hills, is the **Eremo di Camaldoli**, the Hermitage where many of the monks and acolytes reside in modest and quiet solitude. This is the original settlement founded by San Romualdo in 1012 AD.

Next, delve even deeper into these mountains, over to **Badia Prataglia**, a small town that grew up around a monastic settlement founded in the 10th century, even older than that of Camaldoli. ("*Badia*" is short for *abbadia*, meaning abbey or monastery.) Though the abbey here was eventually disbanded a few centuries later — the monks of Camaldoli evidently had more influence with the Pope at the time — the original 10th century **Church of Maria Assunta** remains intact. Underneath the church lies a crypt dating back to the 8th century. A walk into this dark, rocky space feels like the first few steps into the underworld. Today a beautiful arboretum is carefully maintained where the rest of the abbey once stood. Here, look for the entrance to the **Museo Forestale**, the Casentino Forest Museum. Inside, a series of rooms with elaborate and fascinating displays highlight the region's geography, flora, fauna, and history. Volunteer guides are on hand to offer a tour, though the chance of having an English-speaking one is pretty slim in this remote spot. But even non-Italian speakers will find this museum informative and interesting — and free!

From these remote forest towns of these last two chapters — Badia Prataglia, Stia, Borgo a Mozzano, Barga — various little roads wind their way north into and over the Apennines. They lead travelers towards the vast plains beyond — the breadbasket region of Emilia-Romagna, and yet more Little Roads adventures with fascinating history and great food. You can experience those adventures in our book, *Emilia-Romagna: A Personal Guide to Little-known Places Foodies Will Love*.

Poppi

Albergo San Lorenzo

Charming hotel located just beneath the imposing castle of Poppi. Be sure to book the room with the expansive terrace; its stunning views over the valley are impossible to forget.

Doubles from 69€.

http://www.poppi-sanlorenzo.com

Subbiano

Castello di Valenzano

Gorgeous castle tucked away in the woods; excellent restaurant on site. Very large rooms at a very affordable price.

Double rooms from 70€.

http://www.castellodivalenzano.it/

WHERE TO EAT

Poppi

L'Antica Cantina

Located down a small street in the small town of

Poppi, this beautiful, cozy restaurant has an extensive wine list.

Closed Mondays and November.
http://www.anticacantina.com/

Locanda Fonte allo Spino

Poppi is the nearest town to this Locanda, but it is actually about a 10 minute drive away in the hills. Popular with locals, this restaurant is well worth the drive.

http://www.locandafonteallospino.it/

Valenzano

Ristorante di Castello di Valenzano

Located on the grounds of the beautiful Castle at Valenzano, this restaurant specializes in grilling meats over a wood flame. If you stay here as a guest, you'll smell the wood smoke getting started in the early evening.

http://www.castellodivalenzano.it/

Bibbiena

Ristorante Il Tirabusció

Excellent slow food restaurant in the completely untouristed village of Bibbiena. An unmissable eating experience in the Casentino.

Closed Monday for lunch, and all day Tuesday.
http://www.tirabuscio.it/

Papiano Alto

Trattoria Da Loris
One of our favorite meal stops in the Casentino. Wildly popular with locals, Very well made food (you must get the "scottiglia") at absurdly low prices. Of course they don't have a website. Reservations a must as this place is so popular. If you are afraid to make the call yourself, ask your hotelier to place it for you.
+39 0575 583680

Pratovecchio

Bar Scarpaccia
Bar on the way to Locanda Fonte allo Spino well known locally for making their own stellar pro-sciutto.
Closed Friday.

WHERE TO SHOP

Stia

Tessilnova wool merchants
Store carrying all manner of items made from the historically important and beautiful Casentino wool. Wool Museum next door lets you learn all about wool making in this region past and present for a 4€ admittance.

Open every day from 9:30am-1pm and 3:30-7:30, Saturdays/Sundays open till 8:00.

www.tessilnova.com

Camaldoli

Antica Farmacia

Ancient pharmacy on the grounds of the monastery of Camaldoli; some of our favorite liqueurs in the world are made and sold here by monks.

Open 9am to 12:30pm and 2:30pm-6:00pm, closed Wednesdays and Sundays.

http://www.camaldoli.it/il-nostro-lavoro-home/antica-farmacia.html

WHAT TO SEE

Bibbiena

Museo Archeologico

Small but interesting museum beginning in the prehistoric era and ending with the Romans. Etruscan sarcophagi, statuettes, and jewelry comprise the lion's share of the offerings.

Closed Mondays and Tuesdays. Varying hours according to season, for a full list visit their website. 3€ entry fee.

http://www.arcamuseocasentino.it

Porciano

Castle Museum

Porciano is a very tiny hamlet with its castle and just a few buildings — no bars or restaurants. The castle museum illustrates a slice of Casentino farm life, as well as, unusually, Lakota artifacts from North Dakota (brought over by the castle's American co-owner).

Free entry, but donations are encouraged to help fund the museum. Open Sundays only from May to October, 10am-12pm and 4pm-7pm.

http://www.castellodiporciano.com

Poppi

Castello dei Conti Guidi

Important and beautiful castle in the Casentino region, iconic in these parts. Plan at least an hour for your visit, though it could easily merit up to three. Well worth it to climb the bell tower for its commanding views of the valleys below. Open generally 10-5 in the cooler months and 10-6 in the warmer. 5€ entry fee.

www.castellodipoppi.it

Romena

Castello di Romena

Evocative castle with beautiful grounds; be sure to visit the nearby Pieve di Romena.

Open June, September and October Thursday-Sunday from 10am-1pm and 2pm-6pm. July and August open every day from 10am-6pm. 4€ entry fee.

Badia Prataglia

Casentino Forest Museum
Extensive and interesting displays of forest history, flora and fauna, and life in the Casentino. Free entry. July/August open every day from 9-12:30 and 3:30-6; November-June open weekend mornings only; September/October open Wednesday, Thursday, and weekends from 9-12:30 and 3:30-6.

APPENDIX 1

EATING AND DRINKING

The Restaurant Experience

There are a lot of differences between eating in Italy and eating in the States. Here are a few tips on what to expect, and how to enjoy the Tuscan dining experience to its fullest.

Restaurants have many names in Italy: *Ristorante, Osteria, Trattoria,* and *Locanda* are by far the most common.

The first thing that will happen at any restaurant is the *cameriere* bringing bread and asking what kind of *acqua* (water) you would like. This will always be bottled water, and can be *naturale* (flat) or *frizzante/gassata* (sparkling). Don't ask for tap water — this would be like asking for a drink out of the garden hose.

Bread will usually not come with butter or a dish of oil; it is meant to be used to soak up sauces on your plates. You'll see that a per-person *coperto* (cover charge) is indicated on the menu. This is typically a couple of bucks, and is meant to stand as a minimum service charge.

Meals are served in courses:

Antipasti — appetizers

Primi — pastas, soups or *risotto*

Secondi — meat dishes - this will be just meat; if you want a side dish, order a contorni

Contorni — vegetables, potatoes or salad

Dolci — desserts; occasionally this list will include a cheese plate

Cafe/digestivi — coffee (don't get a cappuccino!) or digestive liqueur, like an *amaro* or a *grappa*

Diners are not obligated or expected to order a dish from every course; we frequently skip either the pasta or the meat course. However, if you find yourself in an especially charming or romantic location, settle in for what we refer to as an "epic" meal.

Once you have a table, it's yours for the night. There will be no turnover or pressure for you to leave. It's generally considered very rude to put a bill on the table, so often the service staff is waiting for you at the end of a meal to approach them to ask for "*il conto*" (the bill).

Meals are slow, and there can be a good amount of time in between courses, as they are making your dish from scratch. If you want a faster meal, try a *panificio* (sandwich shop), pizzeria, or bar, or grab a picnic lunch at a grocery store.

Most small-town restaurants are family-owned, and as a result they won't always adhere to their stated schedules. If one of their family members has a baby or a sudden medical need/wedding/vacation, they might not open up as usual. Be ready to improvise.

A note on tipping

After a meal, you'll need to ask for *il conto* (the check), as they won't try to bum-rush you out as they do in the States. Though it's not generally expected, we often leave a little something extra — usually somewhere between 10 and 20 percent — to show appreciation for good service.

Meal times and reservations

While reservations are not generally required, it's a good idea to have them, even in casual restaurants. Reservations can be made the same day, even an hour in advance. Basically you are just reserving a table and getting a head-start on the lunch rush. No ties/jackets are ever required at the places we recommend (though you are welcome to wear them if you like). Some of the restaurants we recommend are real mom-and-pop places, and some are upscale, but all will allow you to eat there wearing regular clothing (no Speedos/flip flops, however).

It's not unusual to make a reservation and then be the only people eating that day. Sometimes the reservation just insures that the restaurant opens at all. In the US if you saw an empty restaurant, you'd know that was a sign of poor quality; but that is often not true in Italy, especially in very small towns. No reservations are required (or even possible) in pizzerias and small sandwich shops; reservations are only for sit-down restaurants.

Seatings for *pranzo* (lunch) generally happen no earlier than 12:30 and no later than maybe 2:00. Shoot for 1:00-1:30 to be safe. If you're looking for a place to eat at 2:30, you may be totally out of luck.

Cena (dinner) starts at maybe 7:30, and goes on until everyone is done eating. Again, if you wait much later than 9:00, they may turn you away, depending on how busy the place is.

Breakfasts: Some lodgings offer *colazione* (breakfast), which range from a full-service spread of meats, cheeses, fruits and breads to a packet of biscuits and a yogurt cup in the mini-fridge. We almost always skip it altogether; we like to say that if you need breakfast, you didn't do dinner right.

Bar Culture

Italy's main social scene is at the various neighborhood or roadside bars. This is where you get your coffee in the morning (or any time of day, really), your *aperitivo* before lunch, your drinks and such before or after dinner. Ask for a *café* and you'll get the tiny, very strong espresso. *Cappuccino*, with its frothy steamed milk on top, is typical in the mornings only, though they will make you one any time. Sometimes they will shorten the word "cappuccino" to the slang "cappucci".

Other common drinks:
Spritz Aperol (sweeter) or *Spritz Campari* (more bitter) are cocktails with prosecco; Campari and soda; *spremuta* (fresh squeezed orange juice, you'll see a machine behind the bar with a basket of oranges if they have this); café corretto (espresso mixed with grappa); prosecco; and of course wine. At the bar you can also buy a bottle of water (*naturale* for flat; *gassata* or *frizzante* for sparkling), which you can drink there or take on the road.

We've never seen anyone drinking cocktails like a martini or a cosmopolitan, though they could probably make one if requested. In the last few years many bars have begun to offer Italian-made artisanal beers.

The bar is a great place to try a shot of the endless varieties of Italian 'amari', or liqueurs. Ask for "*un amaro*", and just point to the one you'd like to try. Cynar (CHEE-nar) is made from artichokes, Montenegro from herbs, Averna also from herbs… It can be fun to give them a try, each will cost 2-4€. They will probably ask you if you want it with ice ("*con ghiaccio*").

If you order a cocktail (e.g. Aperol spritz, or an *amaro*), the bartender may also bring you a little dish of nuts or olives, tiny sandwich bites or other snacks. Those are free with your drink. If you're happy with the drink and service, it's nice to leave a Euro or two as a tip. (Note: baristas do not generally expect tips, but they always appreciate one.)

Key dining terms

colazione, pranzo, cena — breakfast, lunch, dinner

prenotazione — reservation

tavola — dining table

carta — menu

aperitivo — a little drink before the meal

vino della casa — house wine

bicchiere — glass

bottiglia — bottle

carafe — carafe

barriche — barrel

fuori/dentro — outside/inside ("*Possiamo mangiare fuori?*" "Can we eat outside?")

digestivo — a little drink after the meal

Fatto in casa — made in-house

troppo cibo — too much food

sono pieno — I am full

non posso mangiare piu — I can't eat any more

OK, forse solo uno dolce — okay, maybe just one dessert

GENERAL TIPS FOR TRAVELING IN ITALY

Passports

Your US passport must be valid for six months after the last date of your trip. If your passport expires in October and your trip ends in May, you will not be able to board the plane.

If you need a new passport or need to renew your old one, the State Department recommends doing that at least 6 weeks in advance. We recommend 3 months, just to avoid the stress of frantically checking the mail every day. We also highly recommend applying for Global Entry, which will greatly expedite your time waiting in line at both ends of your trip.

Renting a car

International Driver's Licenses are required for foreign drivers in Italy. These can be purchased at AAA (even for nonmembers) for $15. You will also need your regular driver's license.

Snow tires or chains are now legally required between November 15 and April 15. This will often mean an additional fee from the rental company (to hire chains) if the car is not equipped with snow tires. You may not see any snow (we rarely have, after multiple winter trips) but nevertheless you are required to pay to be prepared. If you know it is going to snow, or if it starts to snow, you need to stop and get the chains on. Having not put chains on a car since 1980 or so, we don't love the idea either, but it's a small price to pay for a great trip (and to avoid a citation from the *Carabinieri*, the Italian state police). For more driving tips — from picking up the car to insurance to traffic signs to navigation to parking— check our website, www.LittleRoadsEurope.com, which includes many pictures and links.

Driving in Italy

People are often intimidated by driving in Italy. The drivers are often fast and aggressive, and American drivers may feel pressured to go faster by drivers who tailgate very closely. This is just a cultural norm in Italy — remember that it's not personal. If someone is following you too closely, look ahead for a place to pull over and let them pass easily. Usually they're not even paying attention to you, they just drive like this out of habit. If they are irritated at your slow speed, that's okay— once they pass you, you'll probably never have to see them again. Give them a little wave and cheerful "Ciao!" as they pass you by.

Tolls

The only toll roads are the Autostrada highways. Approaching a toll plaza, you'll see lanes marked in blue that say "*Carte*" (credit cards). You can use your credit card in the automated machines to get through. If you prefer to pay cash, look for the lanes marked with the pictures of money. Some of the toll plazas give you a "*biglietto*" — a ticket, like on the NJ Turnpike — upon exiting, you insert that before inserting your *carta* (credit card) to pay the toll.

Gas Stations

Filling up is usually easy enough, at one of the many service stations along the highways or in towns. Many of them have two lanes, one for "*Servizio*" and one "*Fai da te*" (do-it-yourself). The self-service is a little cheaper, but we usually opt for the service attendant in case there's some trick to the pumps. Ask for "*senza piombo*" (unleaded) or "*diesel*" (diesel), and tell him how much you want — a number of euro, or just "*al pieno*" (full). (And don't forget to say "*per favore*"!) If the weather is bad we usually tip the attendant a couple of bucks. Most of these places take credit cards, and you'll have to go inside their little office to pay. Sometimes the place is set up just like an American convenience store — just note the number of your pump and tell the clerks inside, and they'll ring you up.

Note: On Sundays, many if not all service stations are closed. In this event, some of them have auto-pay machines that take cash and, depending on the specific machine, some types of cards. These can be confusing, and for this reason we always avoid them altogether, making sure that on Saturday we have a full tank.

Money

Cash is king. Nearly all restaurants and hotels accept credit cards, but some still do not, so make sure you know before you buy. Bars will not accept cards — you will always need cash for that. Italians also have a deep love for exact change, and efforts on your part to produce exact change will be appreciated. They also have a love of small bills. Trying to buy a 1€ espresso with a 20€ note will garner you some dirty looks, and in small towns, they may not even have enough change for that.

Note: We've found that many places that do accept cards do not accept American Express, since their commission fees are so high. Mastercard and VISA are generally fine.

Check with your bank about international ATM withdrawal fees. We use ATMs (*"Bancomat"*) there as needed, as the exchange rate is the same or close to what you will find at the airport. (Traveler's checks have gone the way of wooden dentures, so don't even ask.)

Exchange counters at the airport often offer "deals" that allow you to exchange unspent Euros on your trip back without fees. Alternatively, you can just keep track of your spending in general and work your way down to zero Euros at the end of your trip.

Wi-Fi

Free wi-fi is available at many B&Bs, restaurants and bars. You can call your phone company and have an international data package added for a month. That said, we recommend just using free wi-fi when you find it, or better yet, take a break from constantly being tethered to your phone. You'll be amazed at how much more you experience things around you when you are not focused on staring at a small screen.

Packing

It's impossible to overstate the importance of packing light for a good trip, for two reasons: 1) You want the most mobility and flexibility, so your focus is on experiencing the place you are visiting, and not managing the mound of stuff in your suitcase; and 2) the goal is to arrive with very little, and leave with bags laden down with all the goodies you'll find. Trust us, you'll be disappointed if you can't buy that bottle of oil or ceramic vase because you had to make room for your hairdryer/extra shoes/umbrella. We've traveled overseas dozens of times, and we offer extensive advice on packing smart on our website.

Language

Even in small towns you will often find plenty of English-speakers. Oftentimes you'll find people who want to practice their English by chatting with you. That said, we highly recommend starting your encounters with a bit of Italian. A simple "*buon giorno*" (good day), "*per favore*" (please), or "*grazie*" (thank you) goes a long way. It's easy to learn a few key phrases, and making the effort opens the door for making real connections with people. It's also important to remember that you are a guest in their country, and to treat people the way you would like to be treated.

A note on Visiting/Opening Hours

Opening hours for shops and sites are variable according to the season; but in general, most sites are open from mid-morning until lunchtime, and then reopen from the mid-afternoon until early evening. For most tourist sites (e.g., museums, castles), the last entry is 30-45 minutes before the actual closing time.

On festival days (of which there are many), shops and other businesses may be closed, but most tourist sites will be open (perhaps with varying hours). Look for paper signs plastered on walls for information that you'd normally expect to find on a website; while web presence is increasing, roadside flyers are still the most common form of advertising.

Lodging — What to Expect, What to Look For

Lodging in Italy is much less of the cookie-cutter experience you'll find in the US. In the large Italian cities you can find standard and also luxurious hotels that are like any you would find around the globe. In the smaller towns, though, chain hotels are nonexistent. Instead you'll find small, family run hotels and B&Bs. Sometimes a hotel will be called "Albergo", "Pensione", or "Locanda". A locanda is usually a hotel with a restaurant. B&Bs usually mean you'll have breakfast included, but that breakfast will never involve the eggs, waffles, bacon, and cinnamon buns that you would find at an American B&B. Italians eat very light breakfasts — we always say that if you need breakfast, you didn't do dinner right. At a typical B&B breakfast you'll find coffee, juice, breads (fresh or packaged) and jams, nutella, and maybe yogurt. We almost always skip these breakfasts and instead opt to eat at a nearby bar with the locals, where we take in the sights, smells and sounds of the day. If you intend to eat hotel breakfast, be sure to check if your B&B or hotel offers it free — sometimes there is an additional charge.

A few other things you likely won't find in a small town Italian hotel:

- hairdryers, irons and ironing boards, coffee service, room service
- mini fridge (these are becoming more common now, to our delight)
- TV and phone
- Air conditioning
- elevators
- large, nearby parking lots
- 24 hour concierge

Some of these may be there, but they are not ubiquitous as in American hotels.

You *will* find:

- religious art on the walls
- proprietors who live there or quite nearby, and know the area well
- stunning views
- peace and quiet

When we look for lodging, we are always looking for location. Sometimes we'll book a remote castle, which is not near any restaurants — in that case we may have picnic dinners to avoid driving at night, and also to spend the most time possible in a stunning fairytale location. Sometimes we'll book into a restaurant that has rooms upstairs, so we can eat "epic" meals and then roll ourselves up the stairs at the end of the night to sleep it off. Most often we book small, affordable places in or within walking distance to small walled towns, so we can park the car and leave it while we explore the town on foot. We always look for places that are going to give us a memorable, meaningful trip with a minimum of hassle.

A planning note

Many of the small places we list in this book are, to our knowledge, not listed anywhere else. We have made every effort to accumulate and update the information in this book; however, small businesses can shut down or be closed unexpectedly for illnesses, vacations (*"ferie"*), or just because they felt like it.

Many of the places we list have websites and/or Facebook pages; we suggest you confirm their opening days/times before visiting to avoid disappointment. Without limit, we are not responsible for any distress, disappointment, or damage incurred by following this guide.

However, if you do find information that you think could use updating, please let us know by contacting us via our website:

www.LittleRoadsEurope.com

Buon appetitio, e buon viaggio!

Thank you!

We hope you've enjoyed this book. For more information on the places we travel, please visit us at www.LittleRoadsEurope.com.

If you're thinking about a trip to Italy, consider our Itinerary Building Service. We design custom itineraries for clients based on our extensive travel experiences in Emilia-Romagna, Italy's Alpine lakes, Tuscany, and Lazio. (We also plan trips to Ireland!) Based on your preferences, we'll help you navigate these regions, make reservations, visit artisans, and give day-to-day recommendations for a trip that is authentic, immersive, memorable and affordable. Start your vacation before you even leave, and let us do the hard part!

—Zeneba & Matt

Check out our other award-winning Little Roads Europe Travel Guides!

And coming soon: Our newest guide to Lazio — this is the region that includes Rome, but most travelers aren't aware that there's lots to do and see (and eat and drink!) outside of the big city. And we'll be writing the guide from our tiny new apartment in that very region!

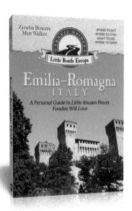

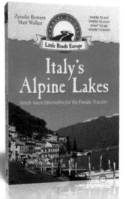

NOTES

NOTES

ACKNOWLEDGEMENTS

Thanks to

Karen-Lee Ryan of Walk Eat Nashville, for her patience and her editing skills;

Robert Firpo-Cappiello of Budget Travel and Nancy Cleary of Wyatt-MacKenzie, for their support and advice;

Laura Atkinson, for her limitless optimism and her map designs;

Kristin Whittlesey, for her unwavering support and encouragement;

brother Dave Walker, for his keen eye and keener expertise;

our visionary friends Sandy Obodzinski and Laura Alabed-Olsson, who first gave us the idea to create Little Roads Europe;

and Andi Bordick, whose essential knowledge, skills, and efforts made it possible to develop our website, our brand, and our business.

Thanks also to the countless chefs, hoteliers, artisans, and guides we've listed in this book, who have inspired us over the years to develop our Little Roads travel philosophy.

CPSIA information can be obtained
at www.ICGtesting.com
Printed in the USA
LVHW011922120919
630924LV00004B/56/P

9 781942 545378